Population and Harvest Trends of Big Game and Small Game Species

CURTIS H. FLATHER, MICHAEL S. KNOWLES, AND STEPHEN J. BRADY

*A Technical Document Supporting
the USDA Forest Service Interim Update of the 2000 RPA Assessment*

U.S. DEPARTMENT OF AGRICULTURE FOREST SERVICE

Flather, Curtis H.; Knowles, Michael S.; Brady, Stephen J. 2009. **Population and harvest trends of big game and small game species: A technical document supporting the USDA Forest Service Interim Update of the 2000 RPA Assessment**. Gen. Tech. Rep. RMRS-GTR-219. Fort Collins, CO: U.S. Department of Agriculture, Forest Service, Rocky Mountain Research Station. 34 p.

Abstract

This technical document supports the Forest Service's requirement to assess the status of renewable natural resources as mandated by the Forest and Rangeland Renewable Resources Planning Act of 1974 (RPA). It updates past reports on national and regional trends in population and harvest estimates for species classified as big game and small game. The trends reported here were derived from State Wildlife Agency biologists and supplemented with data from the North American Breeding Bird Survey for those bird species that are commonly sought by upland game hunters. Big game populations and harvests have generally increased over the 1975-2000 period. Small game populations and harvests, particularly those associated with grassland and agricultural systems, show strong patterns of decline. However, population and harvest trends for both groups need to be interpreted with caution because: (1) not all state agencies reported both population and harvest statistics for all species that are commonly sought by recreational hunters, and (2) there were cases of inconsistent reporting at the species level within RPA reporting regions that necessitated aggregating across species. The trends documented here are consistent with trends documented in past RPA reports completed in 1989 and 1999, although those data were also qualified by the same interpretational caveats that apply to the current report. Trends observed generally among big game species were encouraging, but the continual decline in small game populations and harvest remains an important wildlife resource management issue. Until population and harvest monitoring is improved among institutions that share the stewardship responsibility for recreationally important wildlife, national and regional trends will have to be interpreted carefully.

Keywords: big game, Breeding Bird Survey, harvest trends, population trends, recreational harvest, recreationally important wildlife, small game, State Wildlife Agencies, wildlife assessment

Authors

Curtis H. Flather Research Wildlife Biologist, U.S. Forest Service, Rocky Mountain Research Station, Fort Collins, CO.

Michael S. Knowles Information Systems Analyst, Anadarko Industries, LLC, Fort Collins, CO.

Stephen J. Brady Wildlife Team Leader, Central National Technology Support Center, Natural Resources Conservation Service, Fort Worth, TX.

Acknowledgments

This work was funded by the Resource Use Sciences staff in support of the Forest Service's national assessment reporting requirements mandated by the Forest and Rangeland Renewable Resources Planning Act. This report benefited from constructive reviews received from Stephen C. Torbit, Senior Scientist at the National Wildlife Federation and Kent Cavender-Bares, Senior Research Associate at The Heinz Center. We also wish to thank the Natural Resources Conservation Service (NRCS) State Biologists who coordinated the data compilation and the State Wildlife Agencies who cooperated with NRCS requests for population and harvest statistics.

Contents

Introduction

The American public derives substantial recreational value from the nation's wildlife resources. In the most recent National Survey of Fishing, Hunting, and Wildlife-Associated Recreation (U.S. Department of the Interior, Fish and Wildlife Service and U.S. Department of Commerce, Census Bureau 2006), 12.5 million hunters spent 220 million days outdoors and had direct expenditures totaling more than $22 billion in 2001. Big game and small game hunting were the two most popular forms of hunting, with 10.7 million and 4.8 million participants, respectively. Over the 1996-2006 period, the number of big game hunters has remained statistically unchanged, while the number of small game hunters has declined substantially (–31 percent) (U.S. Department of the Interior, Fish and Wildlife Service and U.S. Department of Commerce, Census Bureau 2006:33). A number of factors could be affecting participation rates in hunting activities (see Cordell and others 2004; Flather and others 1999), including demographics (e.g., an aging population), socioeconomics (e.g., number of persons living a rural lifestyle), access restrictions (e.g., the availability of places to hunt), and wildlife population status.

This report updates recent trends in the population and harvests of big game and small game species that have been compiled to meet the Forest Service's requirements to assess natural resources as mandated by the Forest and Rangeland Renewable Resources Planning Act of 1974 (RPA). Not only will these trends potentially offer some insights into the noted participation trends in the hunting of these species, but such data are also fundamental to documenting resource status as specified in the RPA legislation. Furthermore, big game and small game include species that occur in a diverse set of habitats and therefore collectively provide a representative picture of harvested species that inhabit forest, grassland, and agricultural systems across the nation.

Methods

As is the case with many, if not most, wildlife species we lack standardized, statistically designed inventories to support broad-scale evaluations of status and trend in populations and harvests of big game and small game species. Even the Big Game Inventory formally conducted by the U.S. Fish and Wildlife Service was developed largely by assembling data obtained from cooperating State Wildlife Agencies. The trends reported here also represent a compilation of data that were obtained from State Agencies. The population and harvest (legal) data for big and small game reported in the 2000 Assessment (see Flather and others 1999) were coordinated through the International Association of Fish and Wildlife Agencies. For this update, the Natural Resources Conservation Service (NRCS), through their State Biologists, coordinated the compilation of population and harvest statistics from State Agency biologists for commonly harvested species within each state.

An electronic form that documented population and harvest trends for selected species from 1975 through 2000 (in 5-year intervals) was provided to each State Bologist along with data compilation instructions (see Appendix). State Biologists requested assistance from State Wildlife Agency contacts to provide updated data for 1995 and 2000 and to confirm historical entries (1975-1990) acquired in previous RPA assessment efforts. Forms were returned electronically and entered into the RPA Wildlife database.[1] Trend data are summarized at both the national and RPA regional (fig. 1) scales.

Big game was defined as primarily large mammal species taken for sport or subsistence. Because of historical convention, wild turkey was also classified as a big game species. Small game species were defined as small-bodied resident game birds and mammals that are commonly associated with upland forest, grassland, and agricultural habitats. Small game species include both native and desired non-native species that were purposefully introduced over broad areas of the United States. Because of reporting differences among states, it was not always possible to attribute data to the species level. In those cases, we report trends for groups of species that were taxonomically or ecologically similar. The species comprising these groups are defined in table 1.

---

[1] Data are available upon request from Curtis Flather (U.S. Forest Service, Rocky Mountain Research Station, Fort Collins, CO 80526, cflather@fs.fed.us).

Figure 1. Forest Service RPA Assessment regions.

Table 1—Definition of species groups for reporting of population and harvest trends.

Group Name	Species
Deer	Species of the genus Odocoileus
Cottontail	Species of the genus Sylvilagus
Hare	Species of the genus Lepus
Squirrel	Species of the genus Sciurus and red squirrel (*Tamiasciurus hudsonicus*)
Forest grouse	Ruffed grouse (*Bonasa umbellus*), spruce grouse (*Falcipennis canadensis*), and blue grouse (*Dendragapus obscurus*)
Prairie grouse	Greater prairie-chicken (*Tympanuchus cupido*), lesser prairie-chicken (*Tympanuchus pallidicinctus*), sharp-tailed grouse (*Tympanuchus phasianellus*), and sage grouse (*Centrocercus urophasianus*)
Western quail	Montezuma quail (*Cyrtonyx montezumae*), scaled quail (*Callipepla squamata*), Gambel's quail (*Callipepla gambelii*), California quail (*Callipepla californica*), and mountain quail (*Oreortyx pictus*)

2

USDA Forest Service Gen. Tech. Rep. RMRS-GTR-219. 2009

The absence of data on species or species groups results from variation in the geographic distribution of species and because of inventory gaps in State Agency databases. Interpretation of trends requires that a consistent set of states provide data for all years for the time period of interest. In an attempt to maximize the number of states contributing to the trends, we first identified those states that provided population or harvest estimates for each 5-year interval from 1975 to 2000. We then identified those states with data reporting gaps over that trend interval. If the data gap was bracketed by state data estimates (i.e., the state provided estimates for the 5-year interval prior to and after the data-gap year), we calculated a simple linear interpolation to fill that gap. Although this procedure assumes a linear trend in population or harvest estimates across the gap year, we felt that maximizing the number of states that contributed information was important to ensure that trends were representative and not disproportionately influenced by data from one or a few states. Even after implementing this procedure, there were cases where some species or species groups had very few states that contributed data over the full 25-year period. Trends based on few states should be interpreted with caution. Trends over the 25-year period were assessed by examining the sum across all reporting states at 5-year intervals. Because the trend of sums can be disproportionately influenced by a single state, we also display the mean trend across all reporting states by estimating a smoothing interpolating spline (Schoenberg 1964; Pollock 1994) through the 5-year interval means using Grapher™ (Golden Software, Inc. 2000).

Given that data quality can vary from state to state making regional inferences uncertain, we supplemented the State Agency data with other inventory sources — namely the North American Breeding Bird Survey (BBS). The BBS was established in 1966 to provide spatially extensive data on the population status of breeding bird species across the continental United States and southern Canada (Sauer and others 2007). The survey is run along more than 4,000 active roadside routes, of which about 3,000 are surveyed each year. Routes occur along secondary roads, are nearly 40 km in length, and are surveyed during the peak nesting season (primarily in June). During each survey, all birds seen or heard during a 3-minute period are counted at 50 stops placed at 0.8 km intervals along the route. These data were used to estimate population trend (estimated as the average annual percentage change) over two time periods: a long term period that matched the data obtained from State Agencies (1975-2000) and a short term period reflective of recent trends (2000-2005). We used the route-regression methodology (Geissler and Noon 1981; Geissler and Sauer 1990), which accounts for differing abilities among observers to detect birds (Sauer and others 1994) and a start-up bias caused by lower counts the first year an observer surveys a route (Erskine 1978). For details concerning the design and implementation of the BBS see Bystrak (1981) and Droege (1990).

Results

We received replies to our data request, through the NRCS State Biologists, from all 50 states. Every state provided some harvest data over the 25-year trend period. A total of 40 states provided population estimates for some species or species groups. We sent a follow-up inquiry to the 10 states that did not initially provide populations estimates to confirm that population data were unavailable for the species of interest. Three states replied and explicitly indicated that their Agency no longer reported population statistics for the commonly harvested species covered in this report. The remaining 7 states did not respond to our follow-up request and we assumed that population data were also unavailable for those states.

Big Game Population and Harvest From State Agency Data

The number of states reporting population data for big game species or species groups varied from a low of 9 (elk) to a high of 31 (deer). Nationally, big game populations have shown substantial increases since the mid-1970s that are surprisingly consistent among species (fig. 2). Over the 25-year trend period, wild turkey has undergone the greatest relative increases (+730 percent). However, even the pronghorn, which showed the lowest relative gain, has increased considerably in the 11 states that have reported population estimates from 1975 to 2000. Deer populations (including both white-tailed and mule deer) have undergone the greatest absolute increase, adding more than 14 million individuals within 31 reporting states over the 25-year period.

USDA Forest Service Gen. Tech. Rep. RMRS-GTR-219. 2009

3

Figure 2. Population trends in selected species and species groups of big game for the nation and RPA regions from 1975-2000 (5-year increment). Trend lines are smoothed interpolating splines through the mean across reporting states. Inset graphic is the trend of the sum across reporting states and only appears when more than one state provided estimates. Number of states providing data is given by "n =". Note changes in the y-axis when comparing among regions.

Black bear

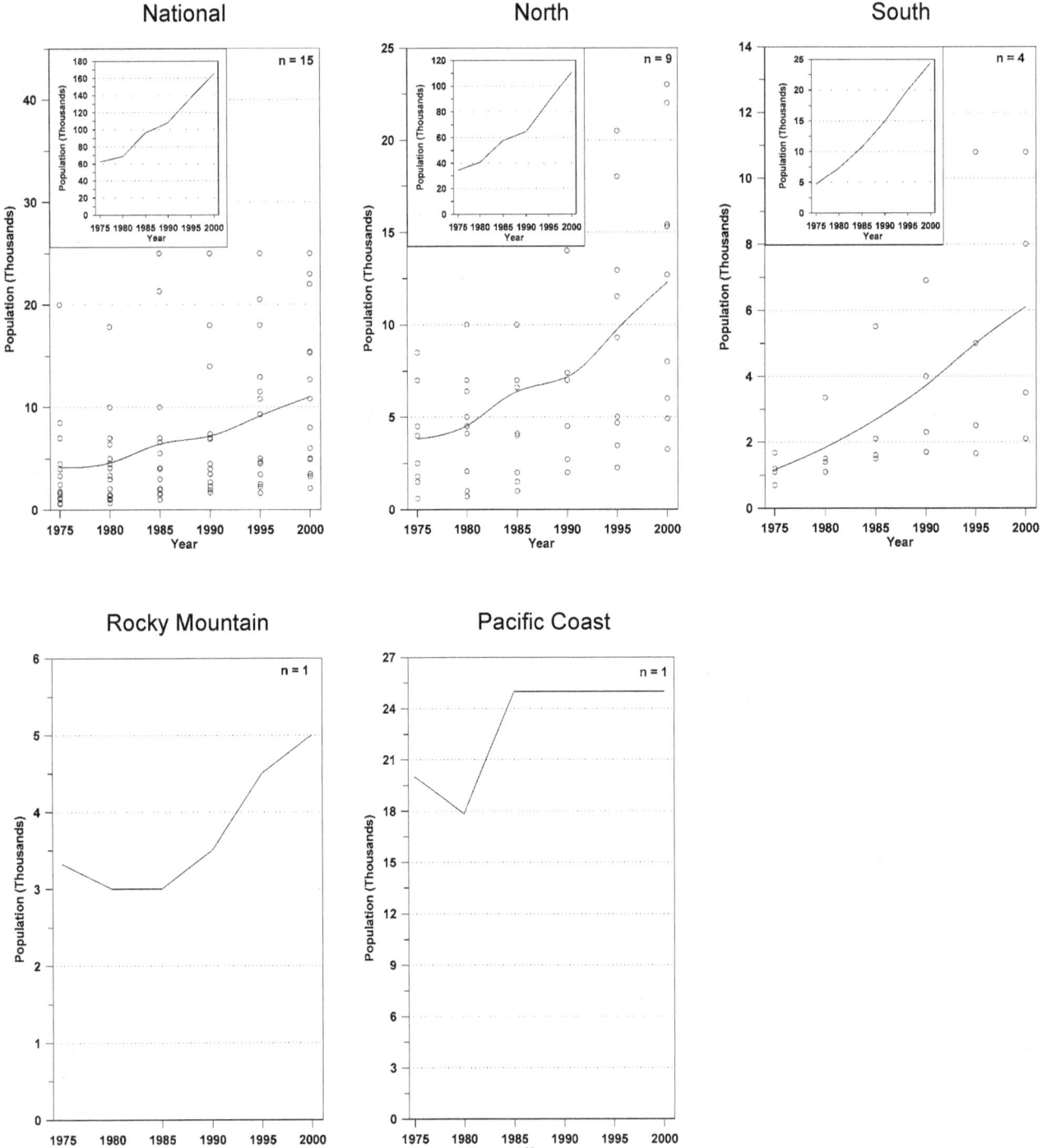

4

USDA Forest Service Gen. Tech. Rep. RMRS-GTR-219. 2009

Figure 2. (Continued).

Deer

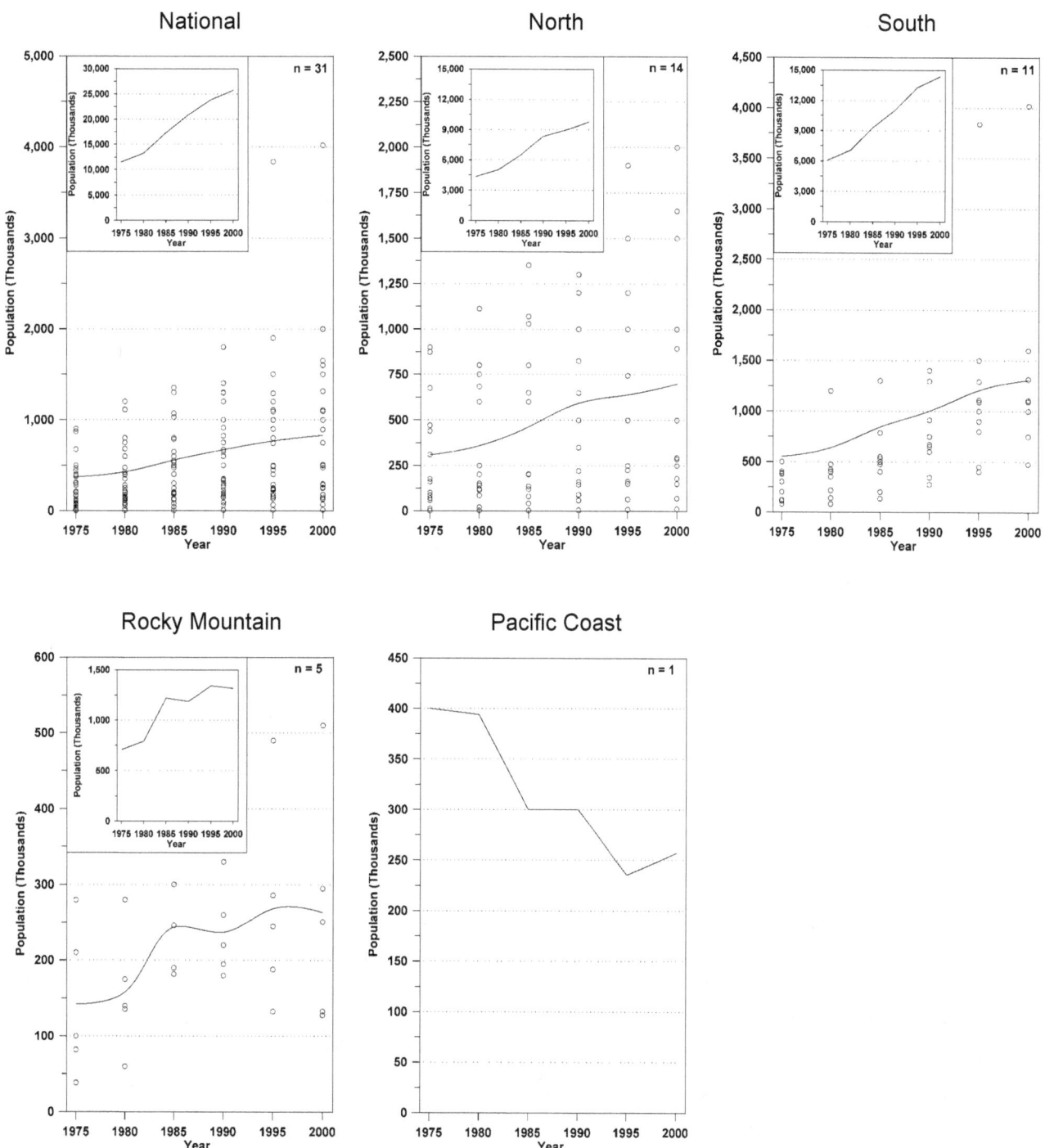

USDA Forest Service Gen. Tech. Rep. RMRS-GTR-219. 2009

5

Figure 2. (Continued).

Wild turkey

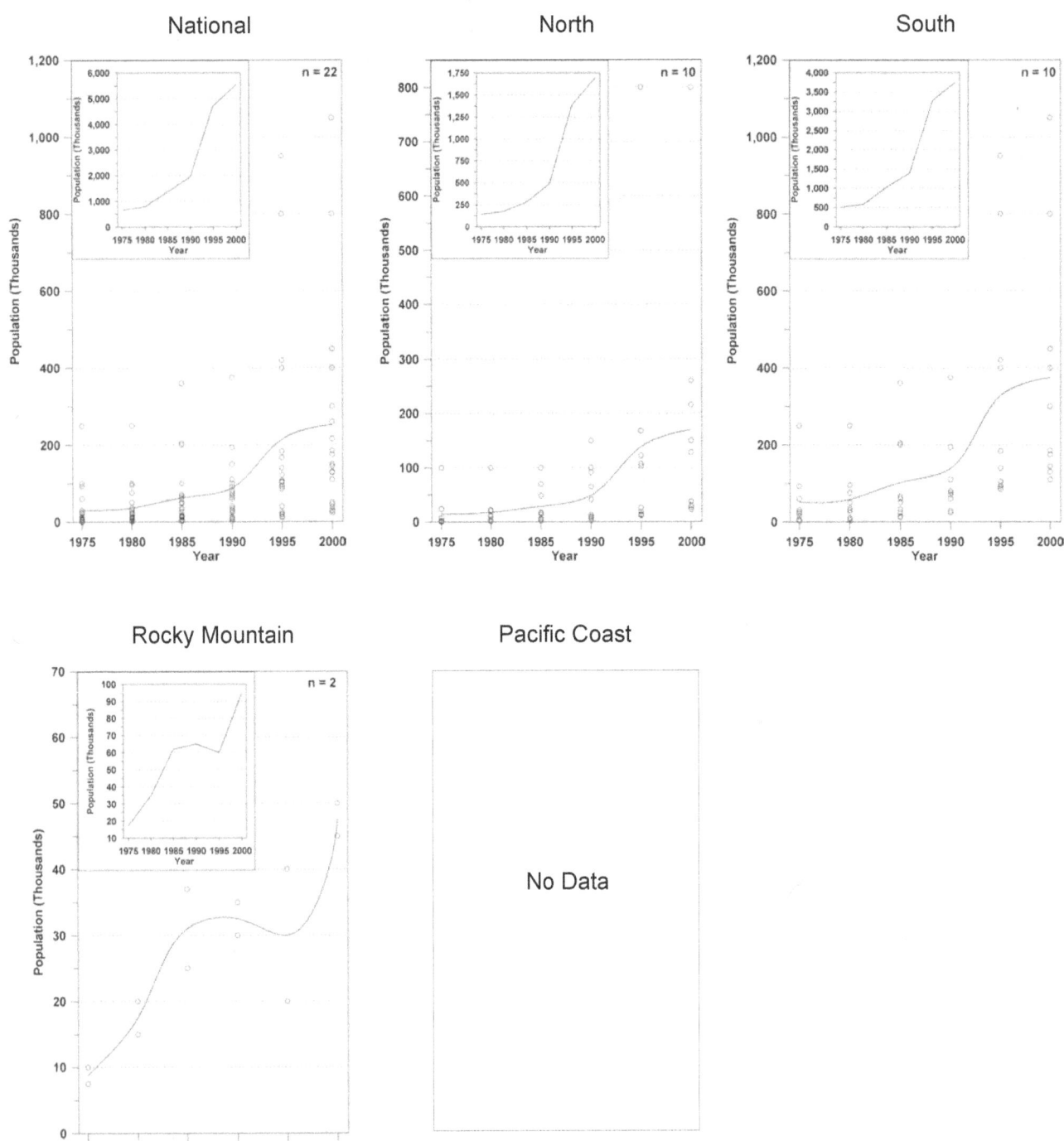

Figure 2. (Continued).

Elk

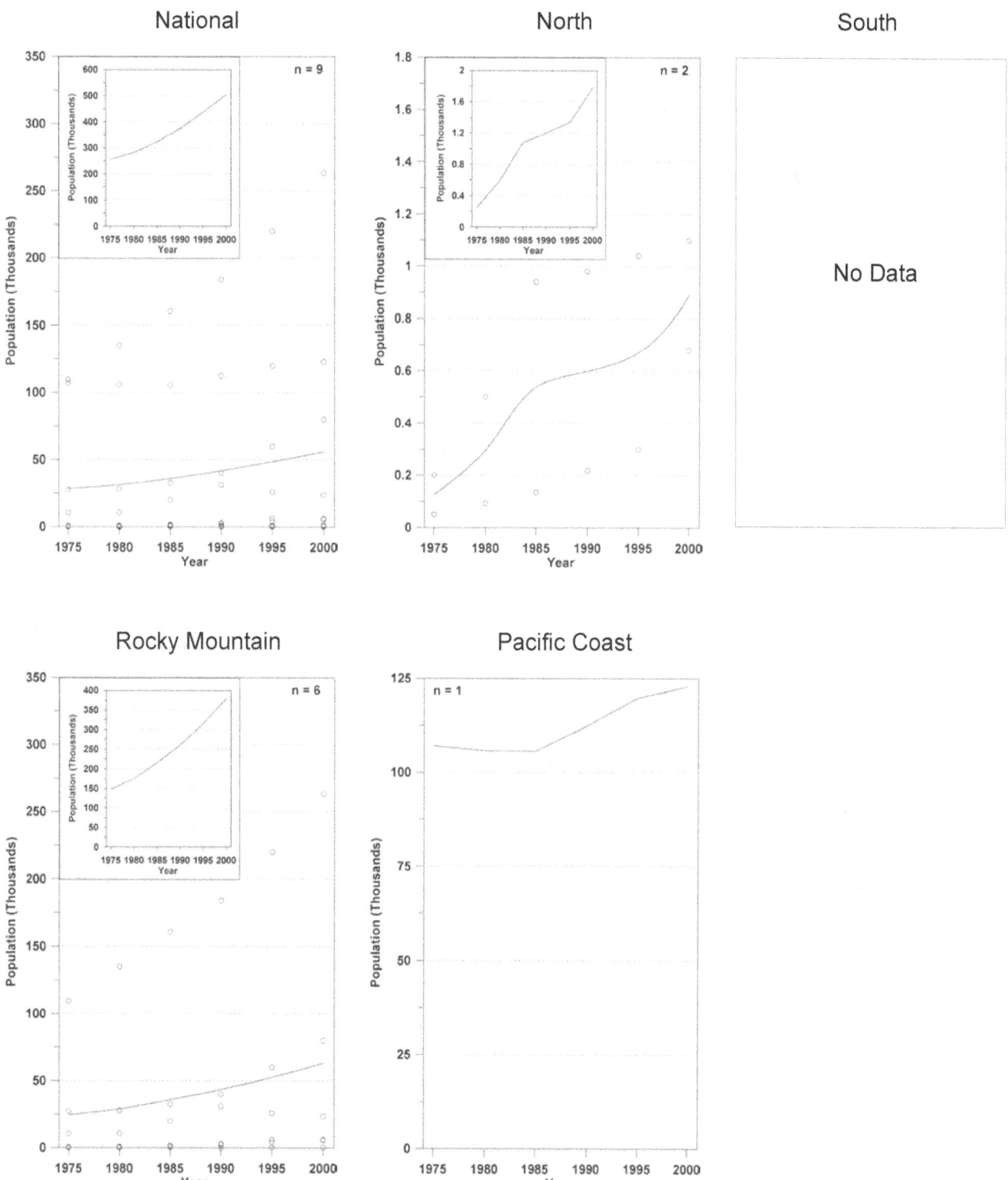

USDA Forest Service Gen. Tech. Rep. RMRS-GTR-219. 2009

7

Figure 2. (Continued).

Pronghorn

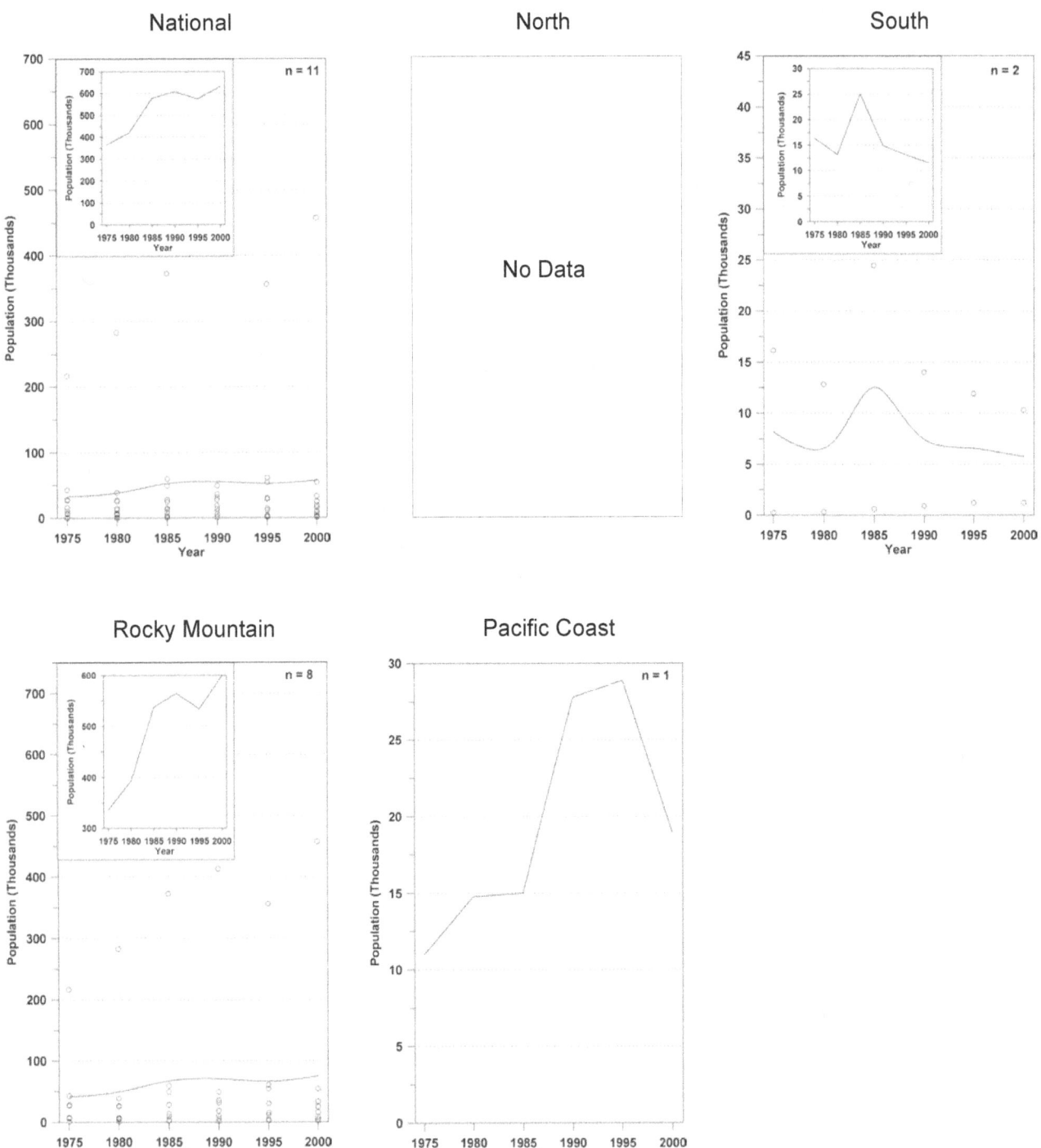

8

USDA Forest Service Gen. Tech. Rep. RMRS-GTR-219. 2009

Figure 3. Harvest trends in selected species and species groups of big game for the nation and RPA regions from 1975-2000 (5-year increment). Trend lines are smoothed interpolating splines through the mean across reporting states. Inset graphic is the trend of the sum across reporting states and only appears when more than one state provided estimates. Number of states providing data is given by "n =". Note changes in the y-axis when comparing among regions.

Black bear

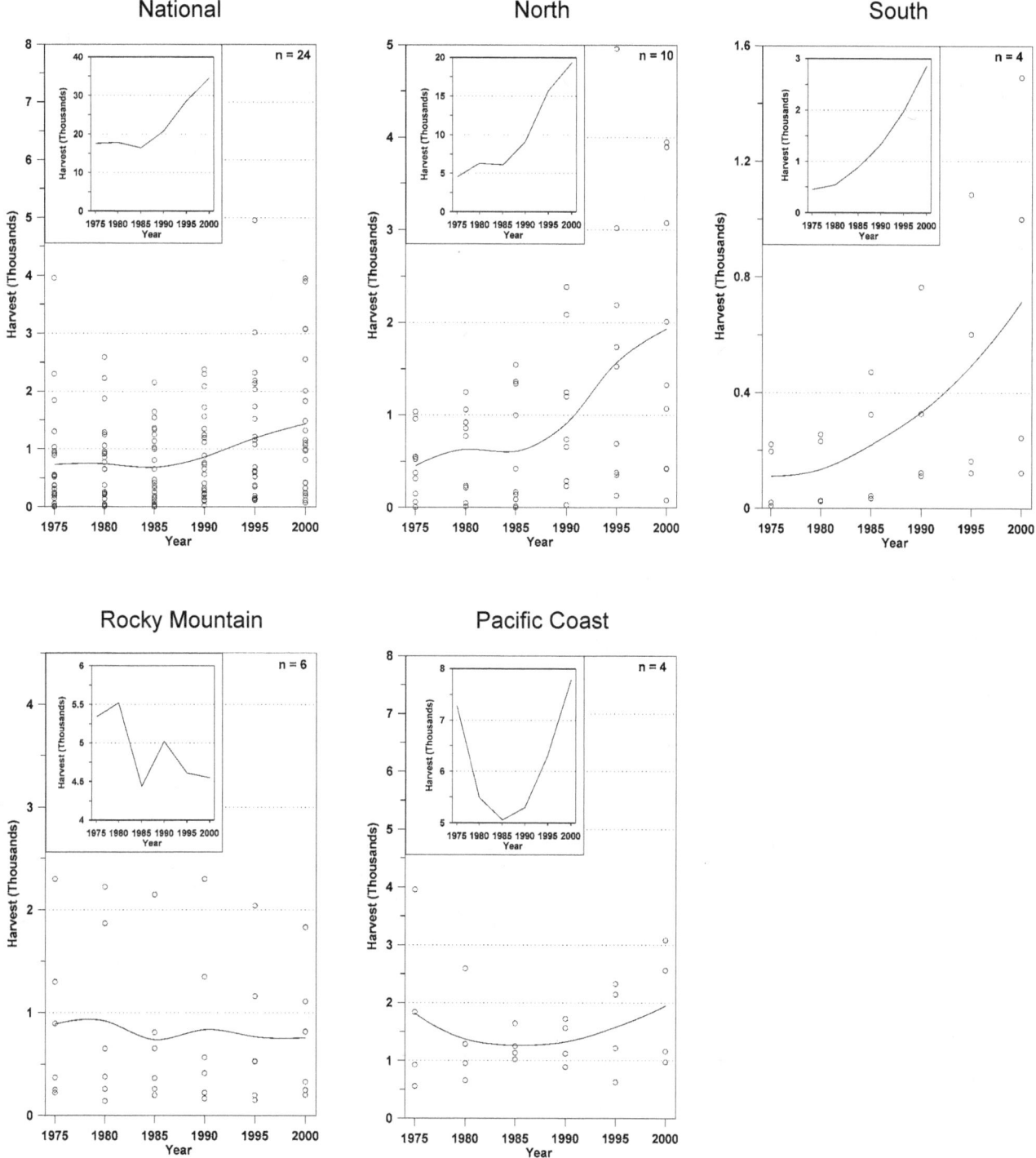

USDA Forest Service Gen. Tech. Rep. RMRS-GTR-219. 2009

9

Figure 3. (Continued).

Deer

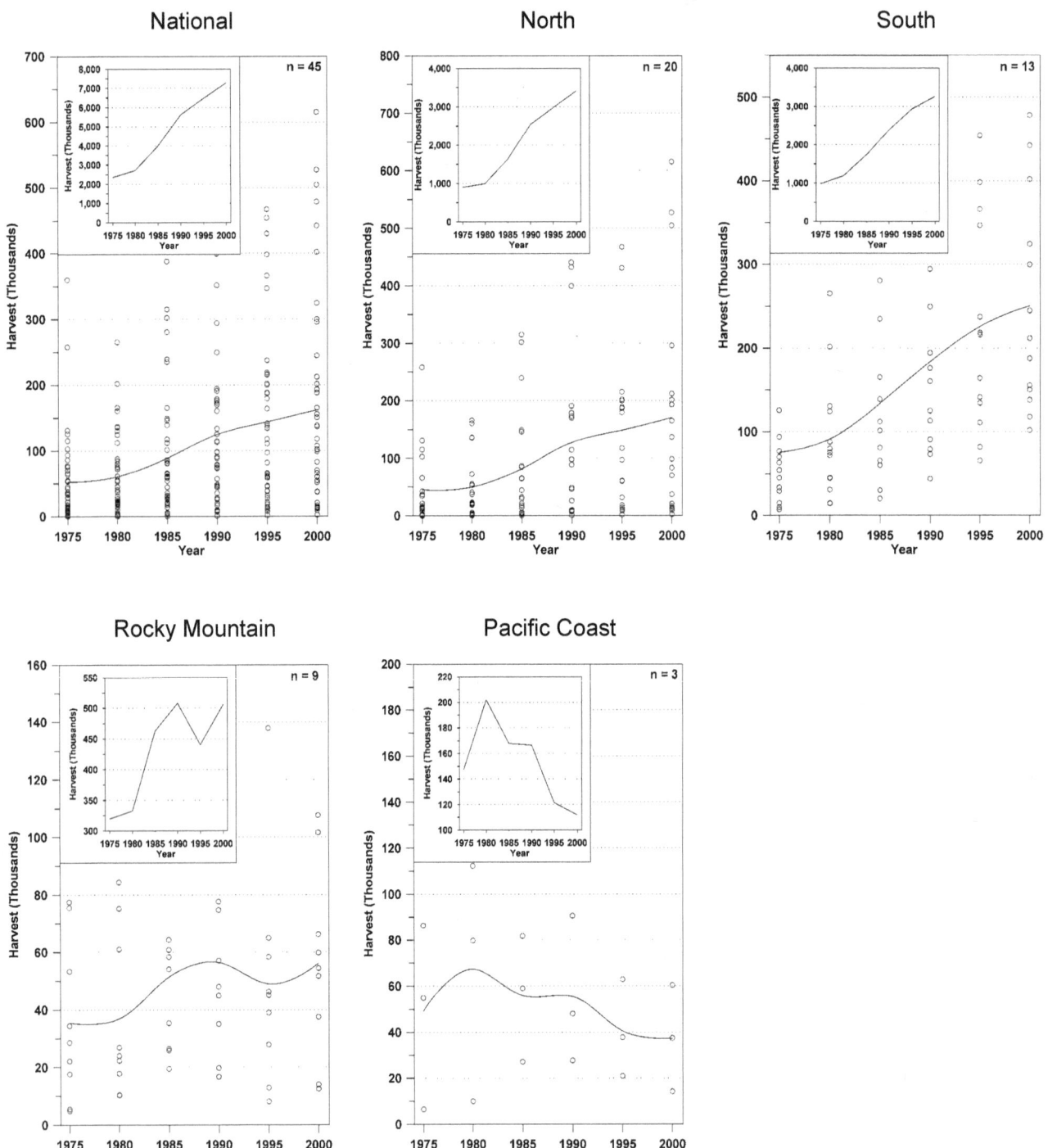

10

USDA Forest Service Gen. Tech. Rep. RMRS-GTR-219. 2009

Figure 3. (Continued).

Wild turkey

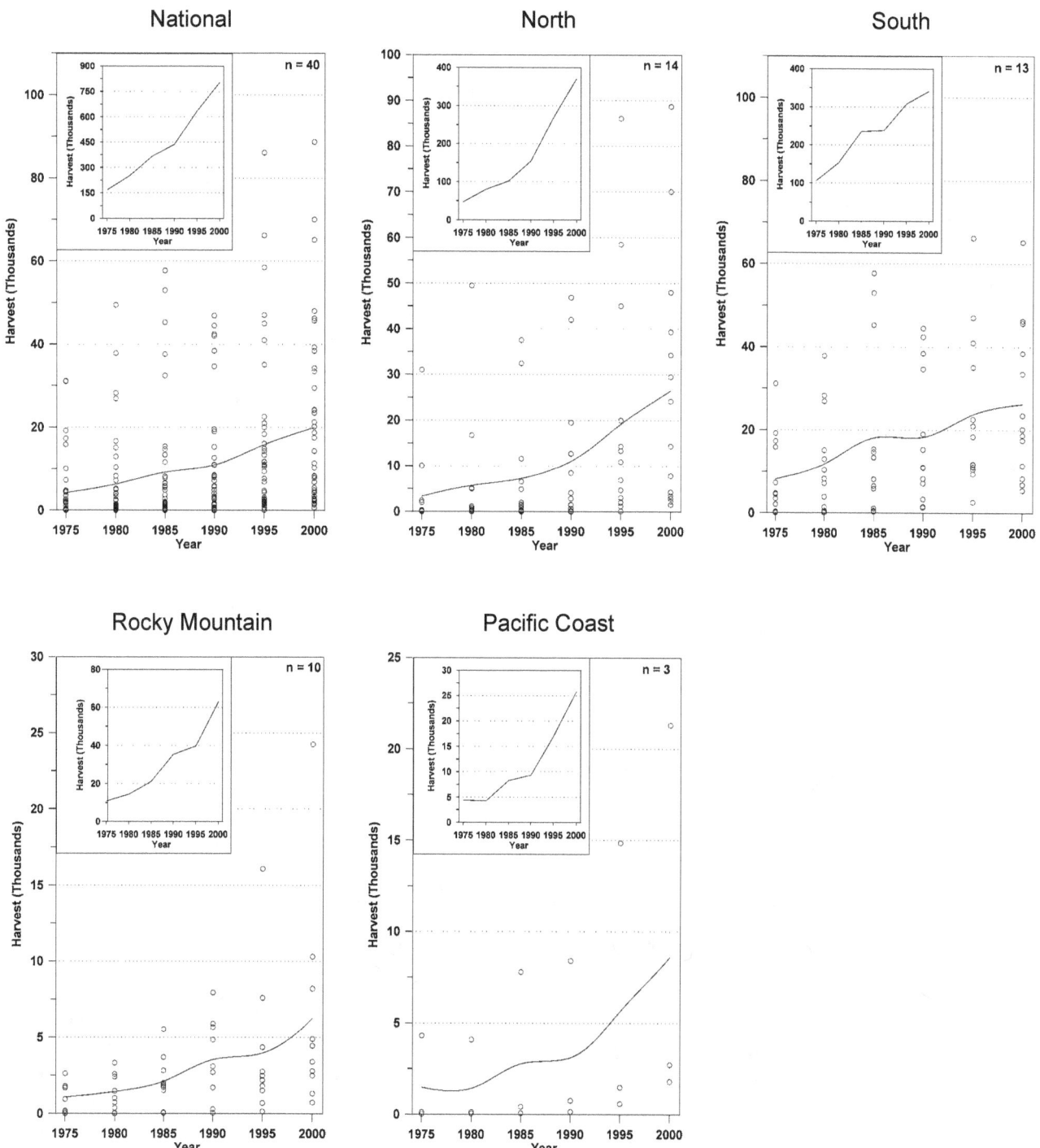

USDA Forest Service Gen. Tech. Rep. RMRS-GTR-219. 2009

11

Figure 3. (Continued).

Elk

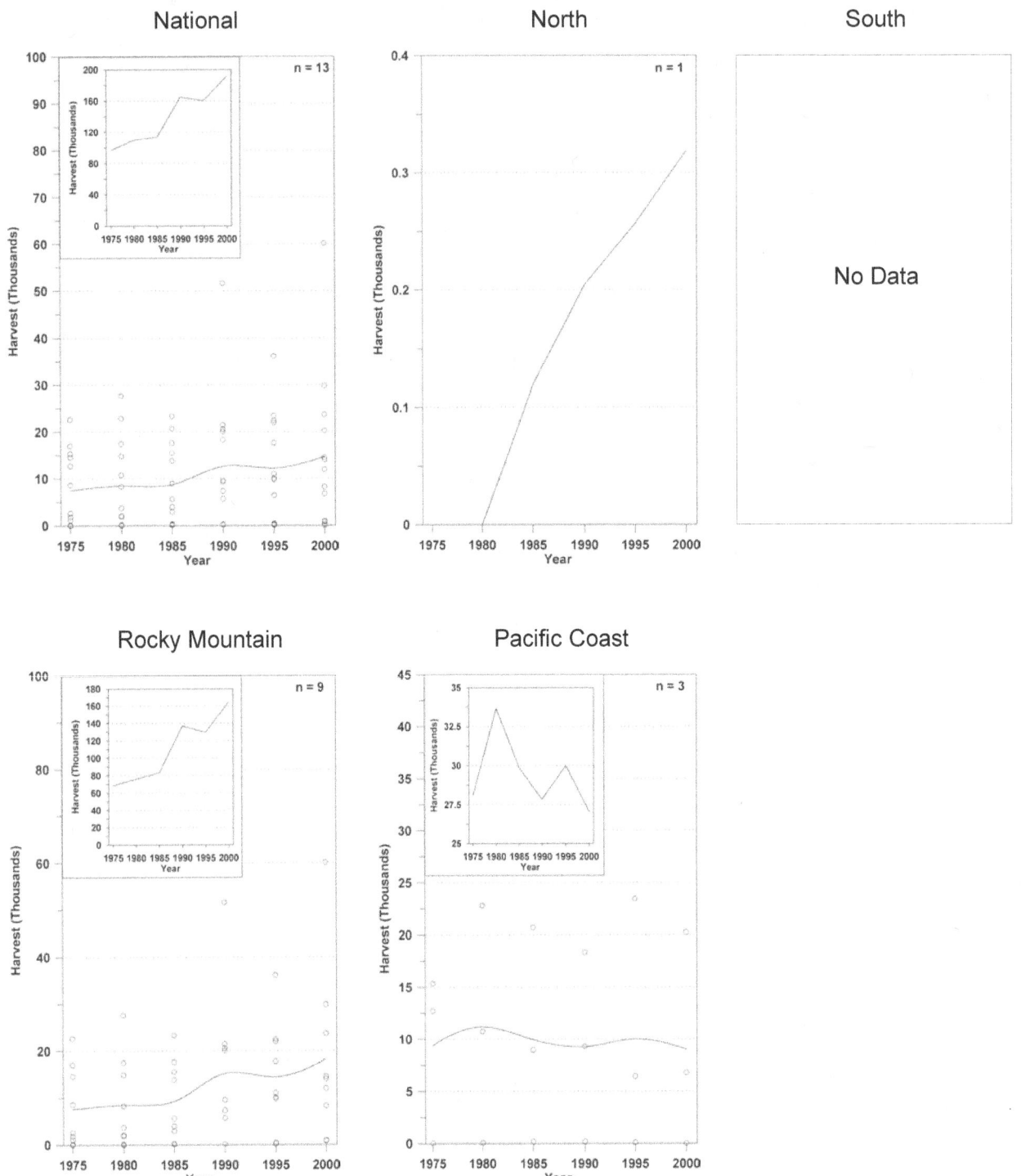

Figure 3. (Continued).

Pronghorn

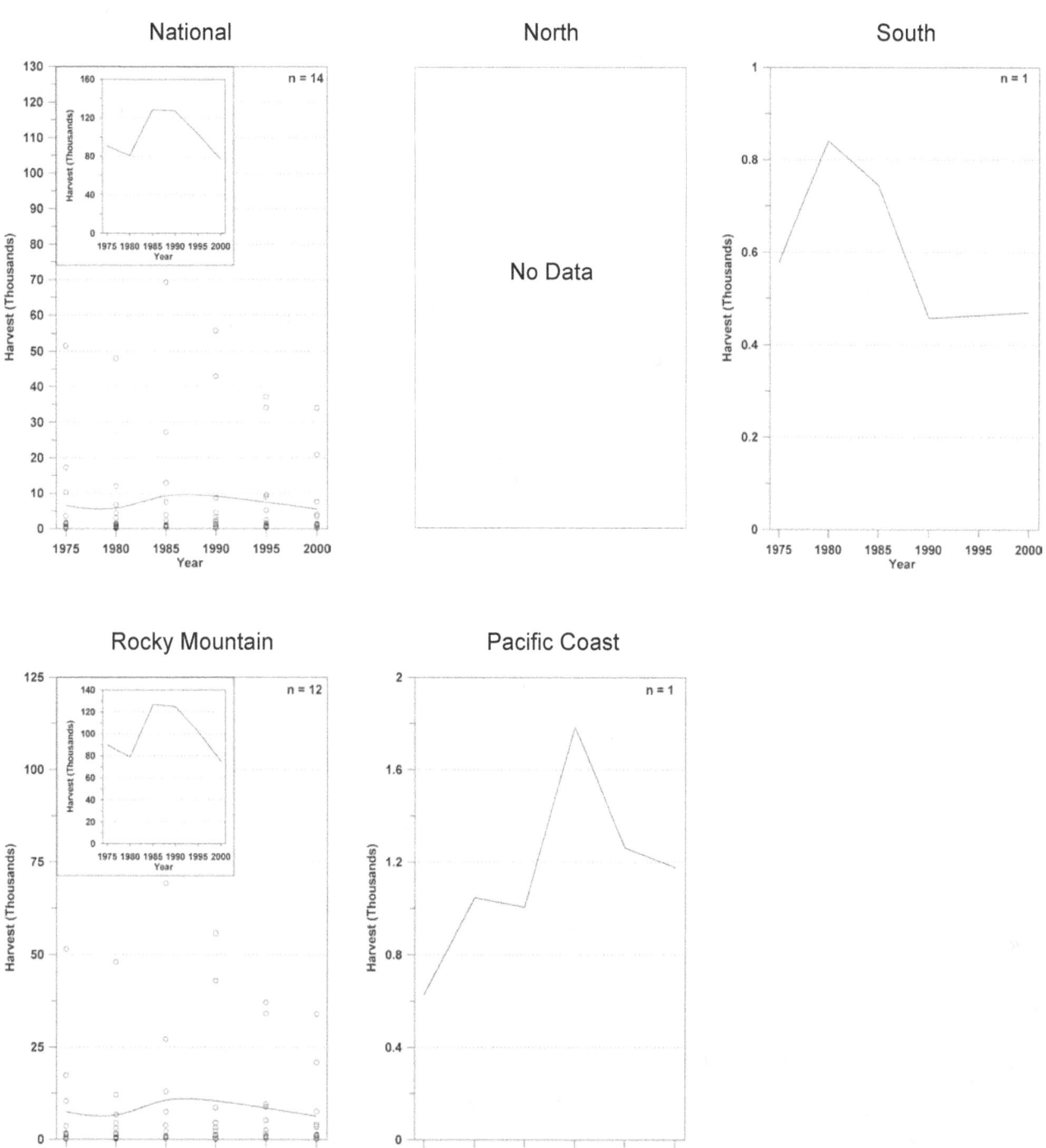

USDA Forest Service Gen. Tech. Rep. RMRS-GTR-219. 2009

13

Figure 4. Population trends in selected species and species groups of small game for the nation and RPA regions from 1975-2000 (5-year increment). Trend lines are smoothed interpolating splines through the mean across reporting states. Inset graphic is the trend of the sum across reporting states and only appears when more than one state provided estimates. Number of states providing data is given by "n =". Note changes in the y-axis when comparing among regions.

Forest grouse

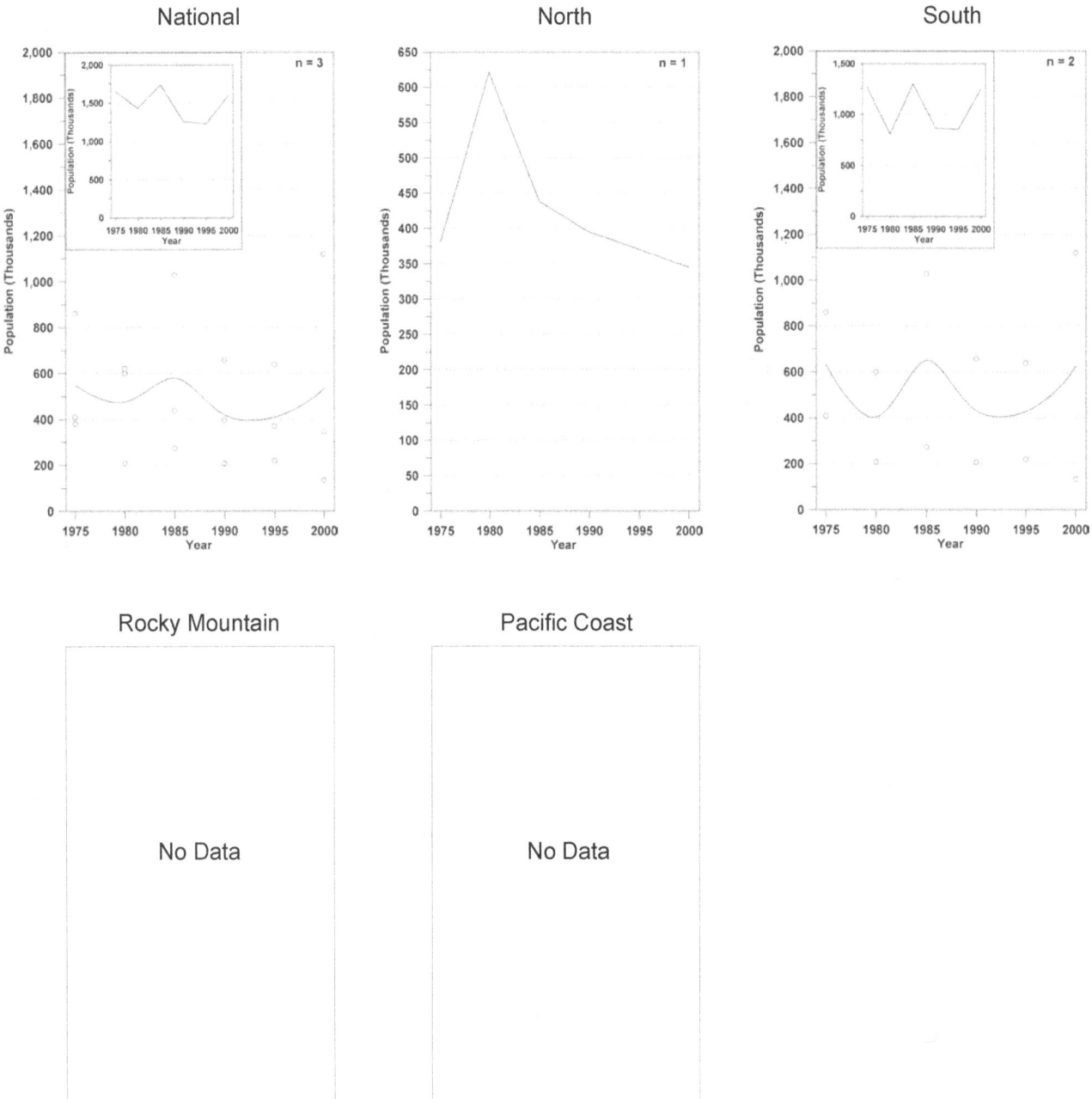

Figure 4. (Continued).

Northern bobwhite

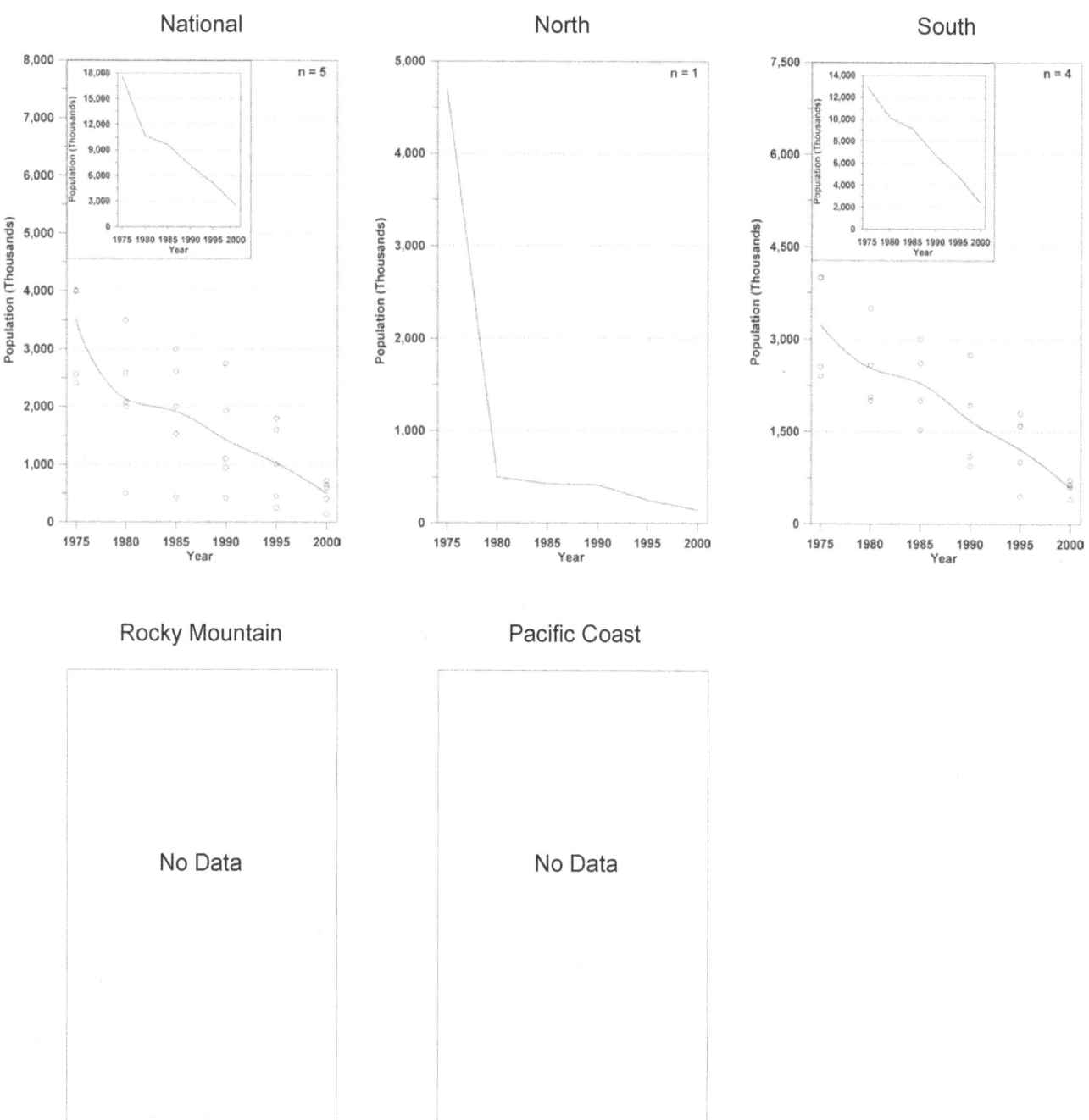

USDA Forest Service Gen. Tech. Rep. RMRS-GTR-219. 2009

15

Figure 4. (Continued).

Cottontail

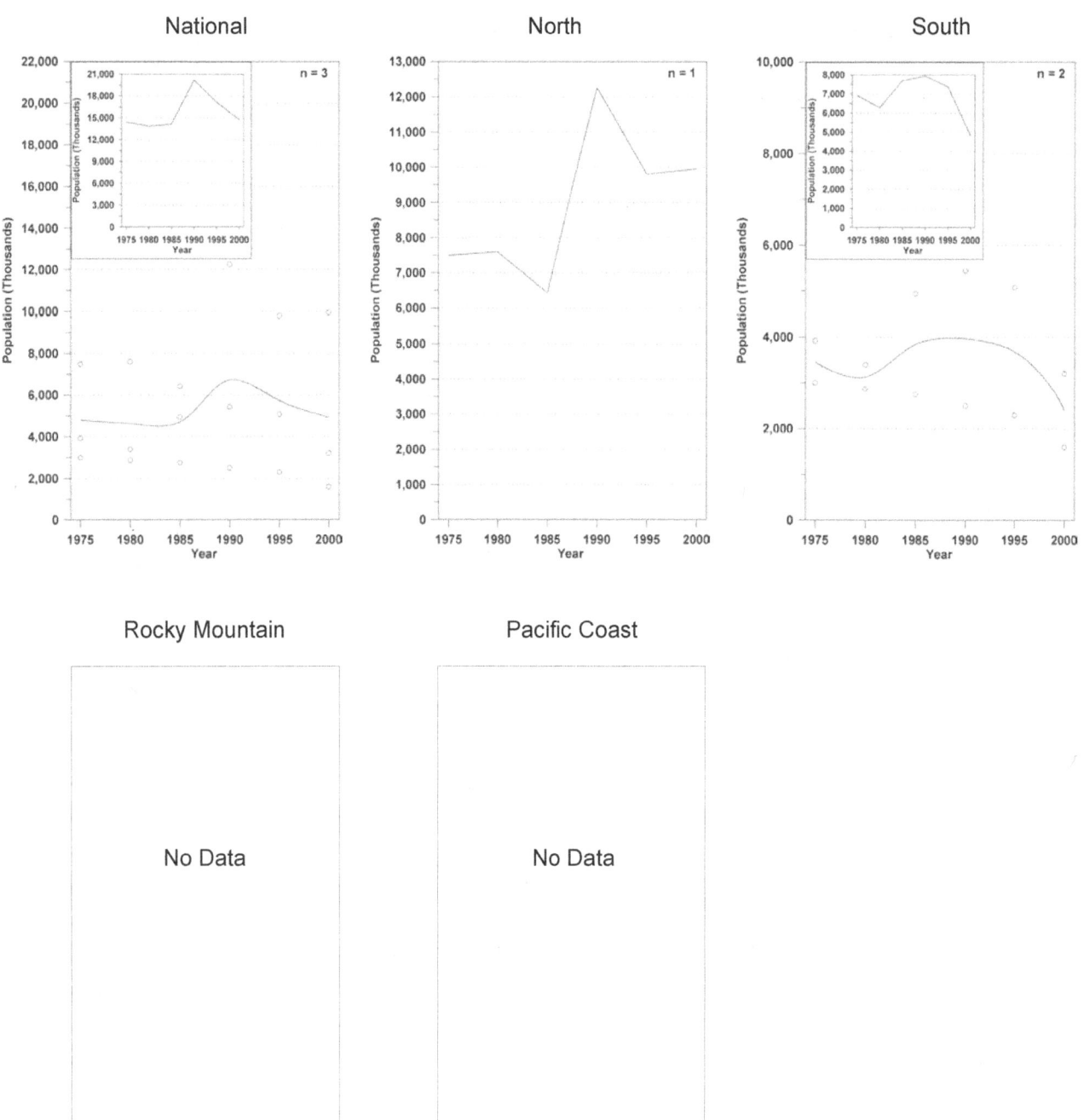

Figure 4. (Continued).

Squirrel

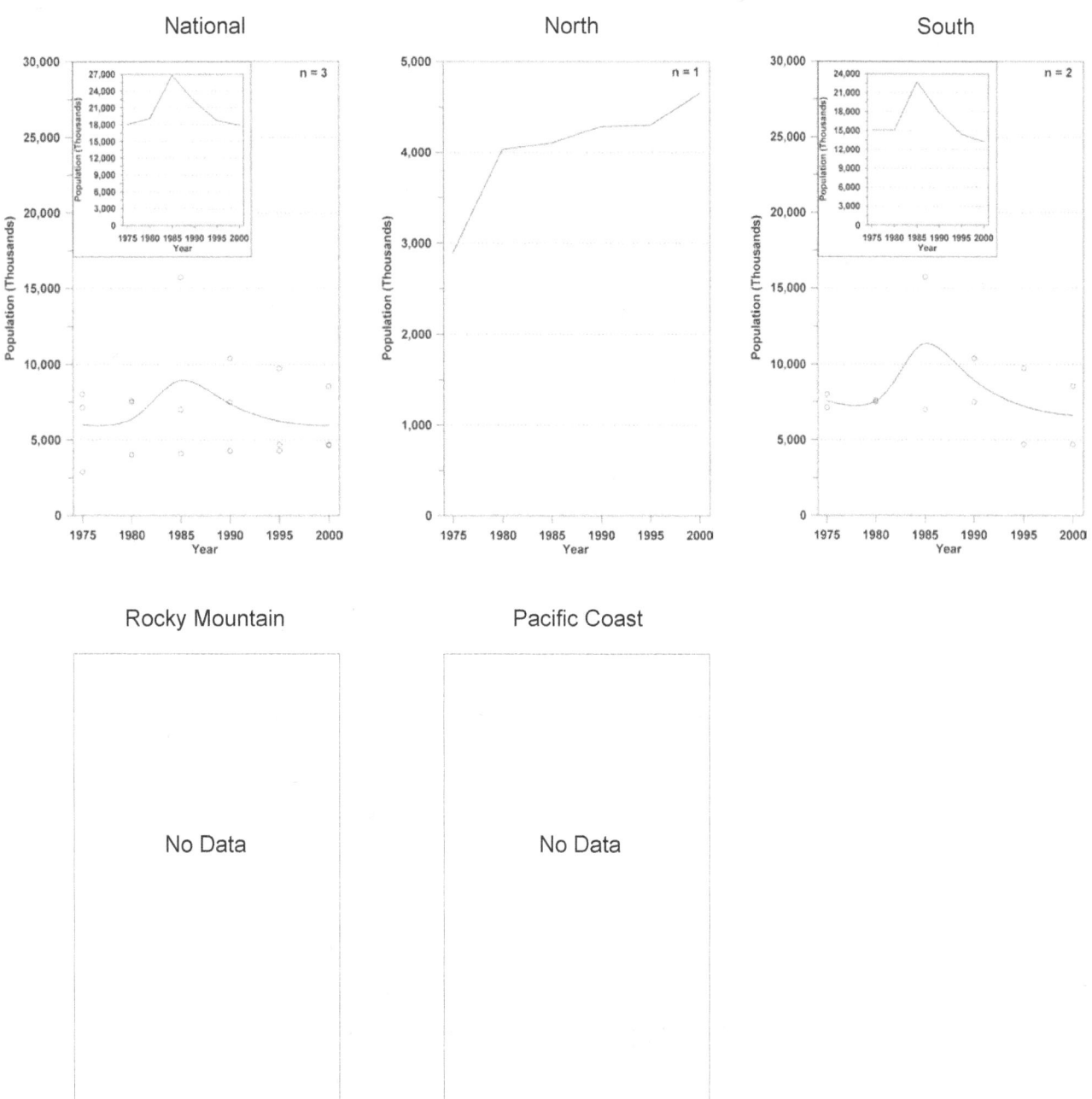

USDA Forest Service Gen. Tech. Rep. RMRS-GTR-219. 2009

17

Figure 4. (Continued).

Ring-necked pheasant

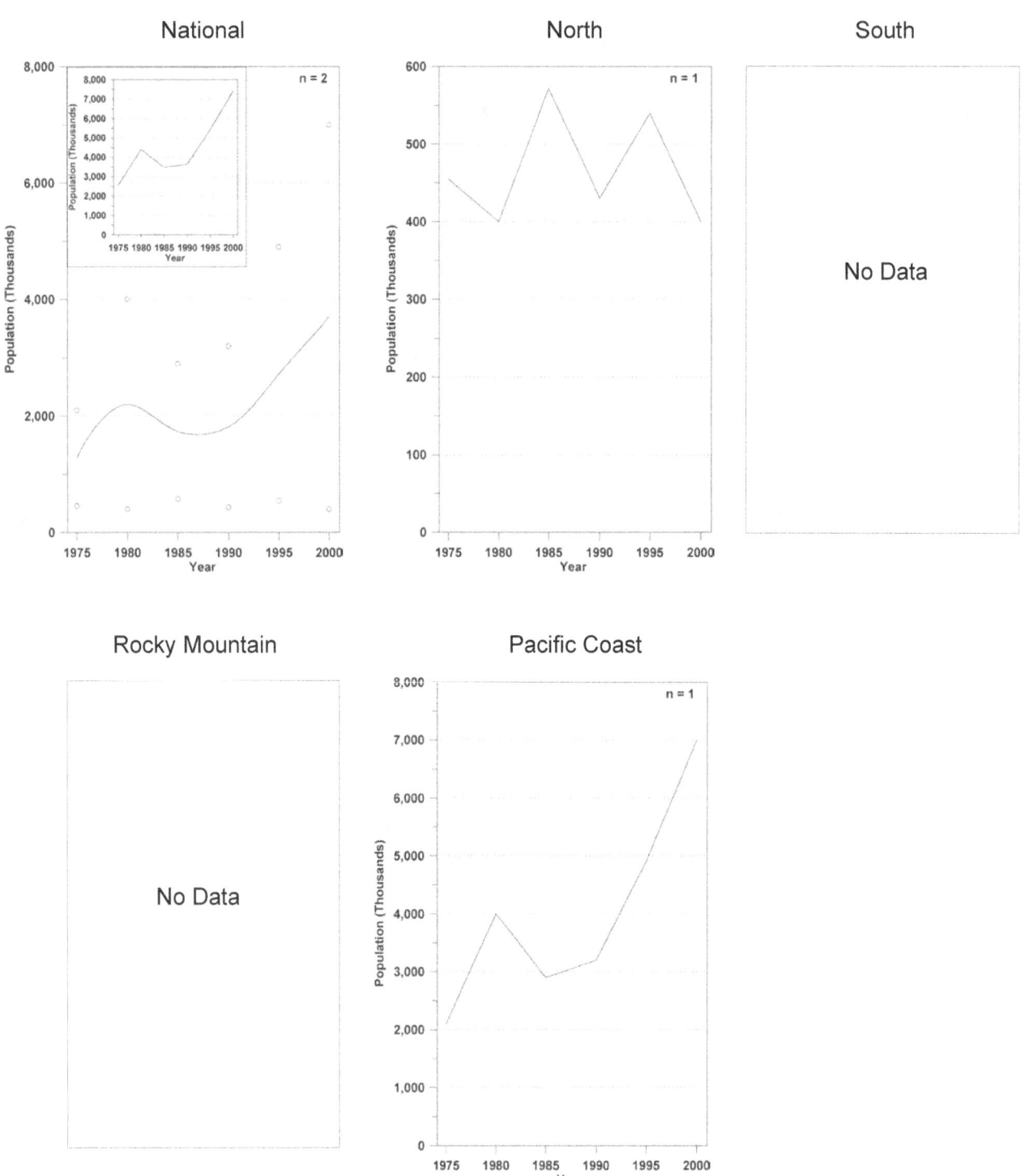

Figure 5. Harvest trends in selected species and species groups of small game for the nation and RPA regions from 1975-2000 (5-year increment). Trend lines are smoothed interpolating splines through the mean across reporting states. Inset graphic is the trend of the sum across reporting states and only appears when more than one state provided estimates. Number of states providing data is given by "n =". Note changes in the y-axis when comparing among regions.

Cottontail

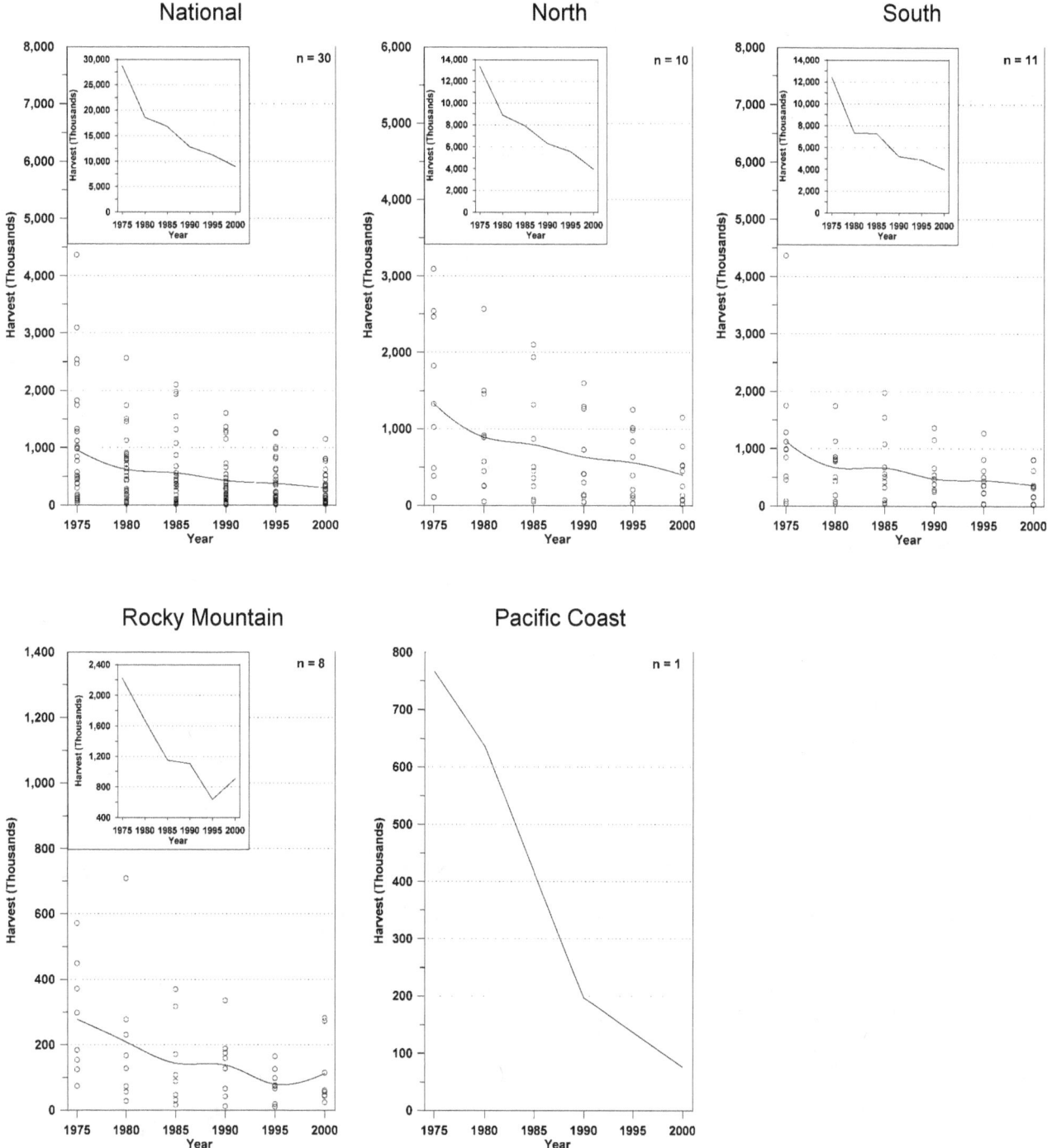

USDA Forest Service Gen. Tech. Rep. RMRS-GTR-219. 2009

19

Figure 5. (Continued)

Squirrel

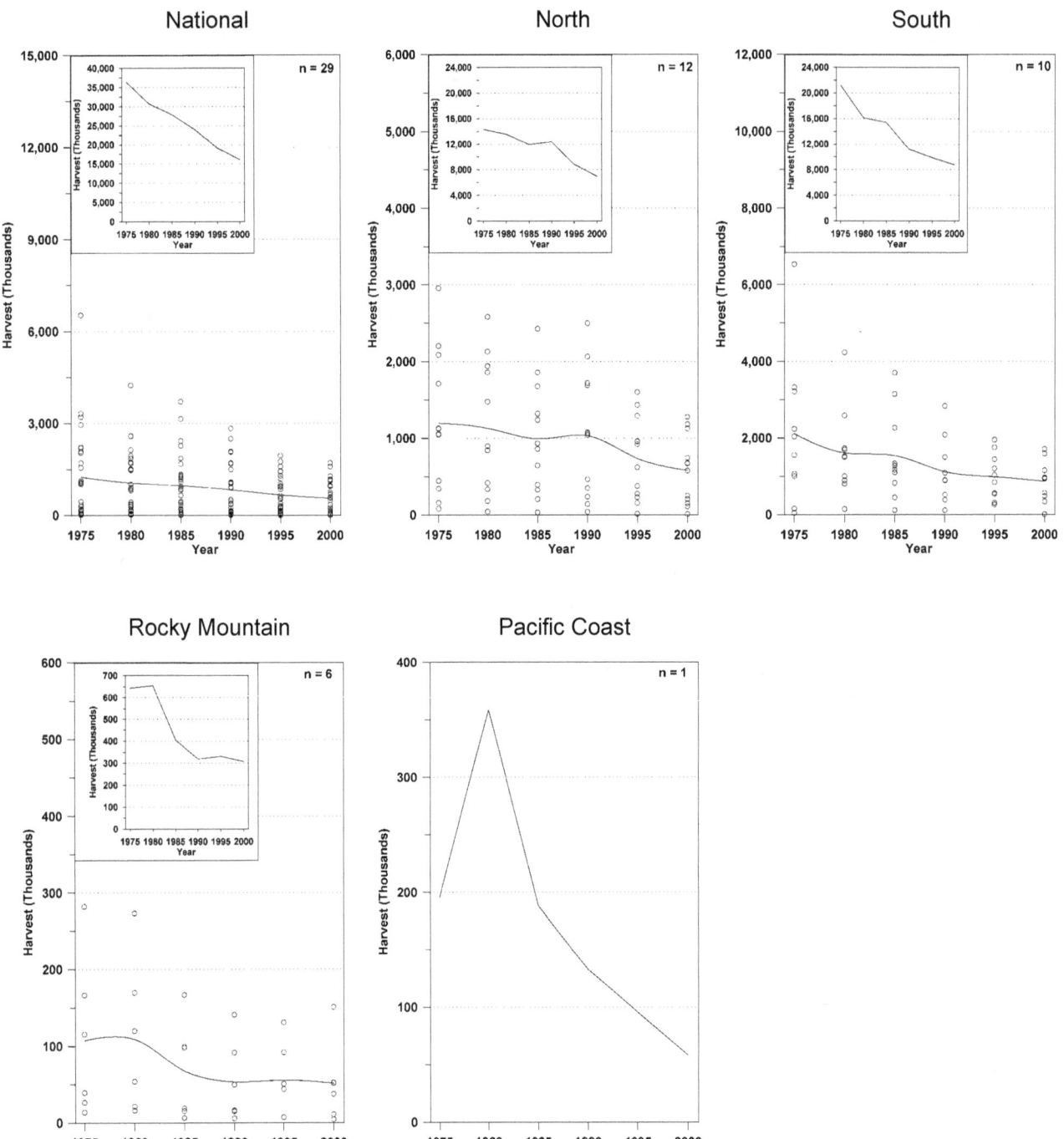

20

USDA Forest Service Gen. Tech. Rep. RMRS-GTR-219. 2009

Figure 5. (Continued)

Ring-necked pheasant

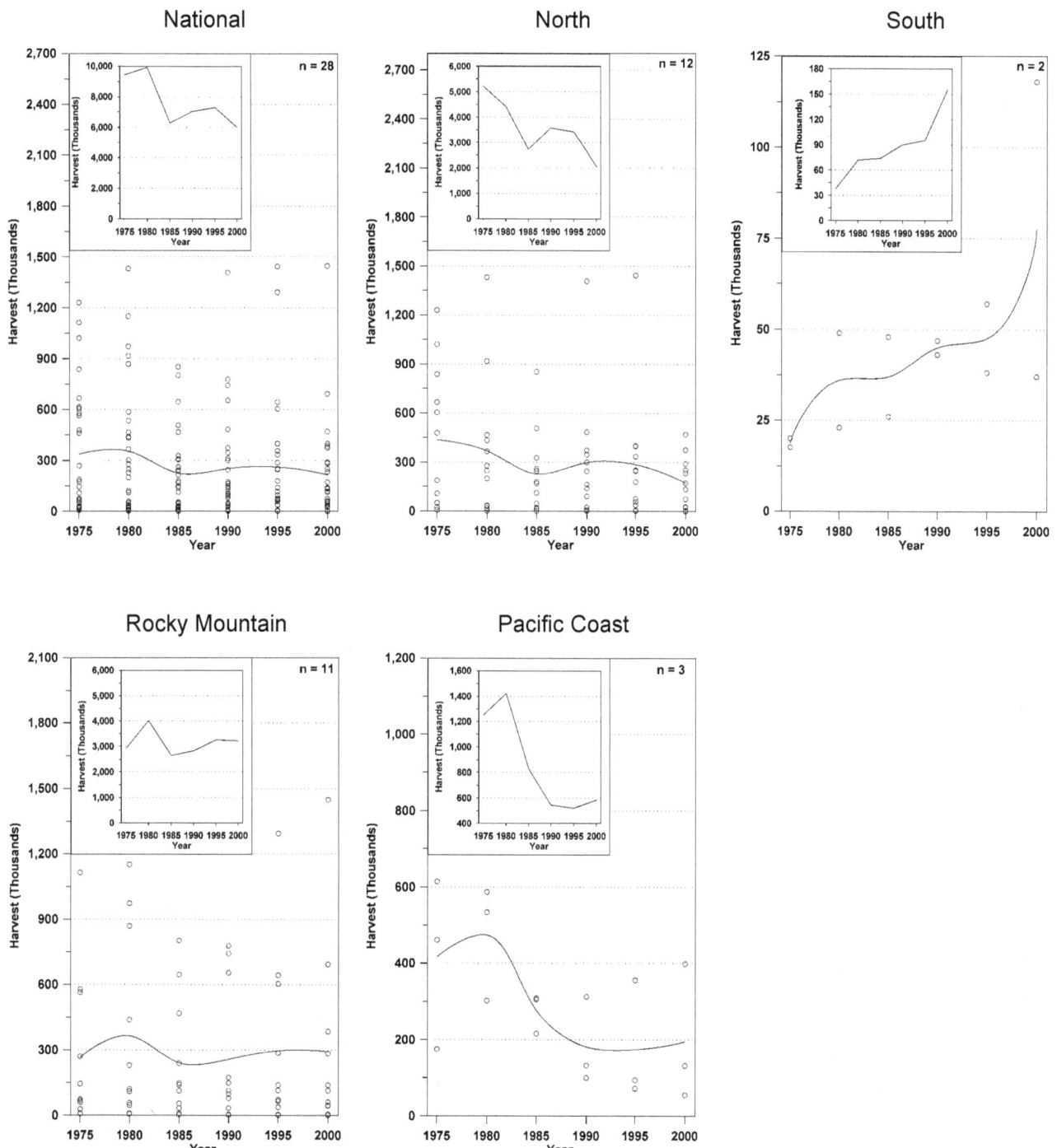

USDA Forest Service Gen. Tech. Rep. RMRS-GTR-219. 2009

21

Figure 5. (Continued)

Hare

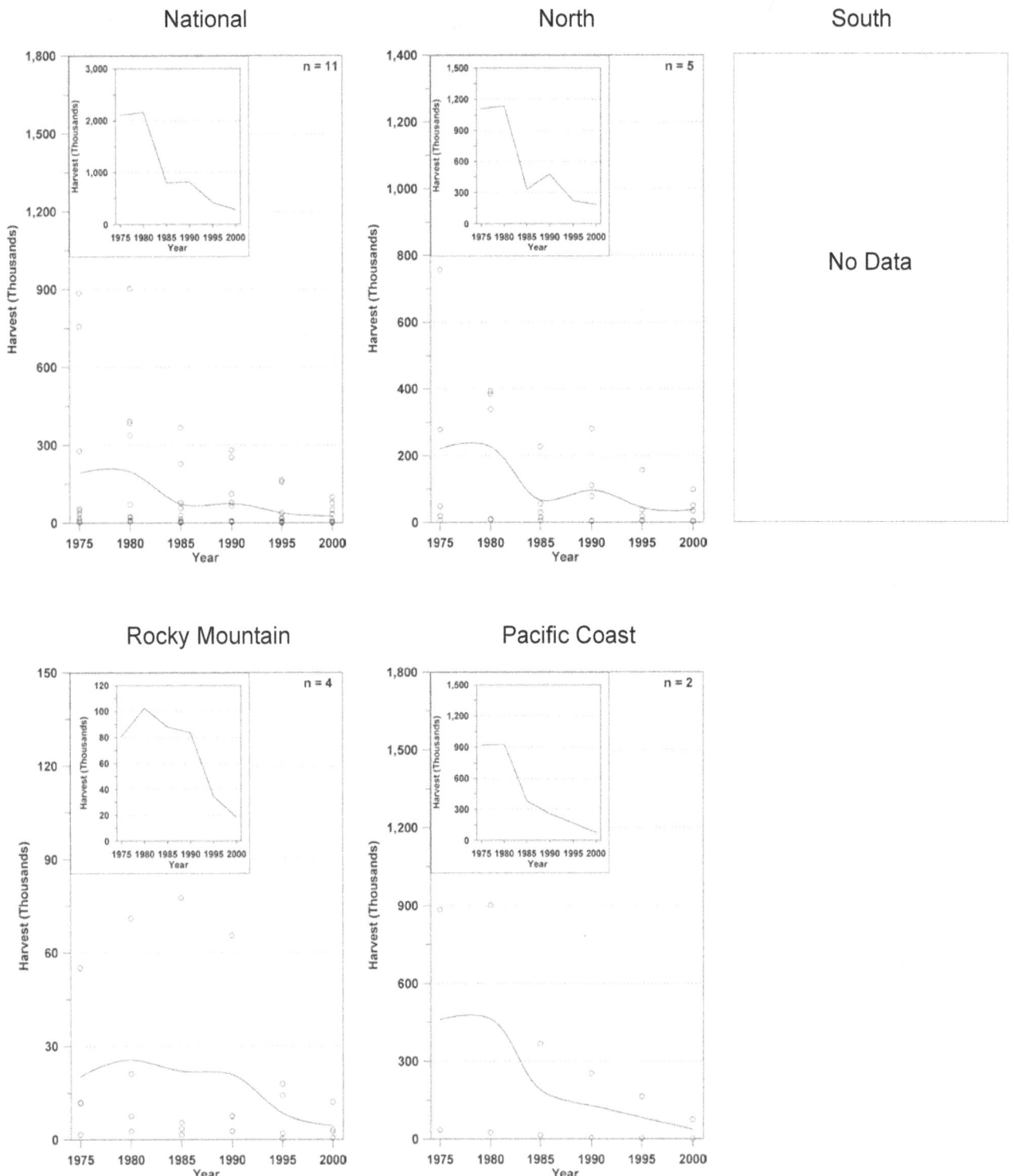

22

USDA Forest Service Gen. Tech. Rep. RMRS-GTR-219. 2009

Figure 5. (Continued)

Forest grouse

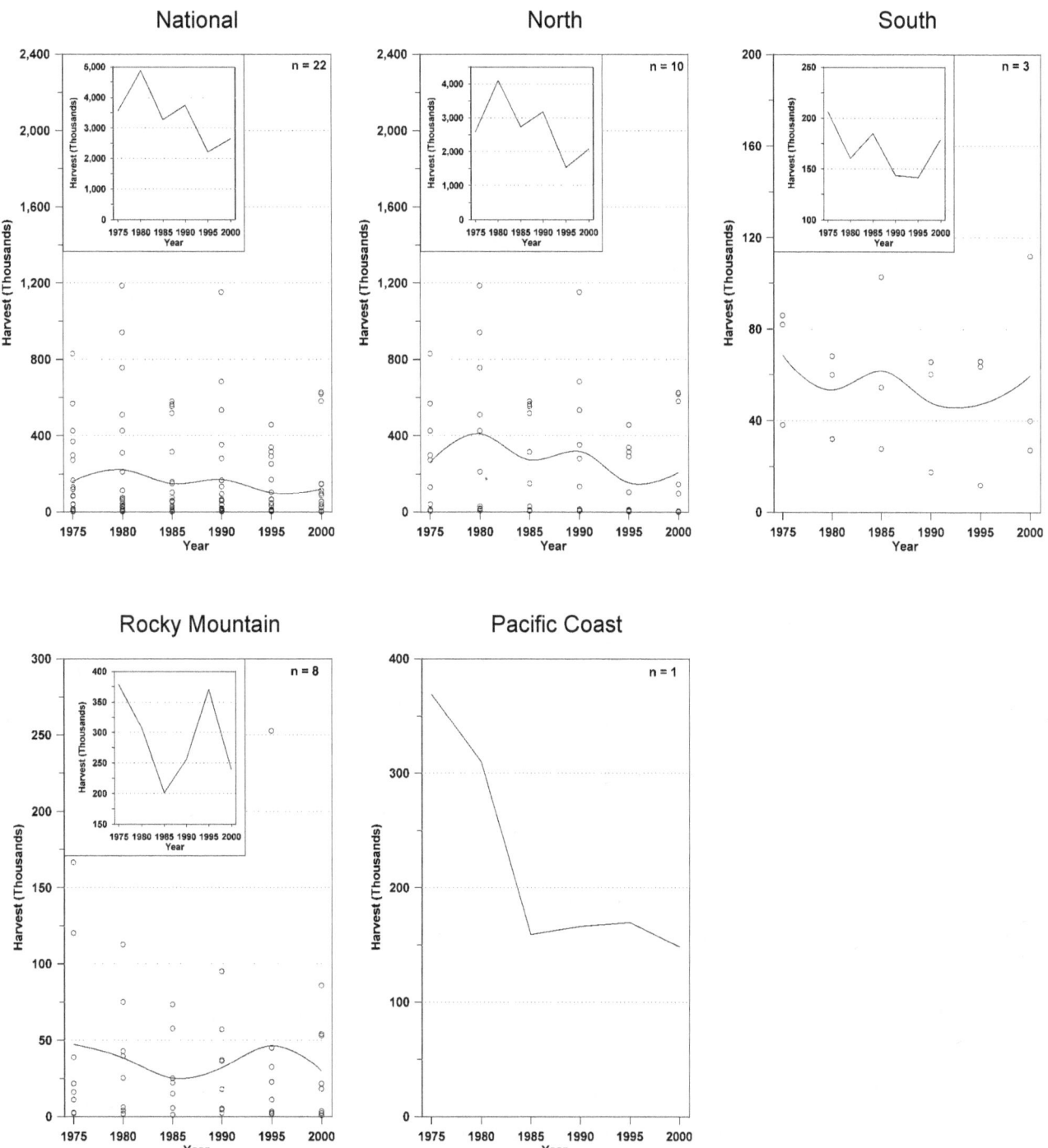

USDA Forest Service Gen. Tech. Rep. RMRS-GTR-219. 2009

23

Figure 5. (Continued)

Northern bobwhite

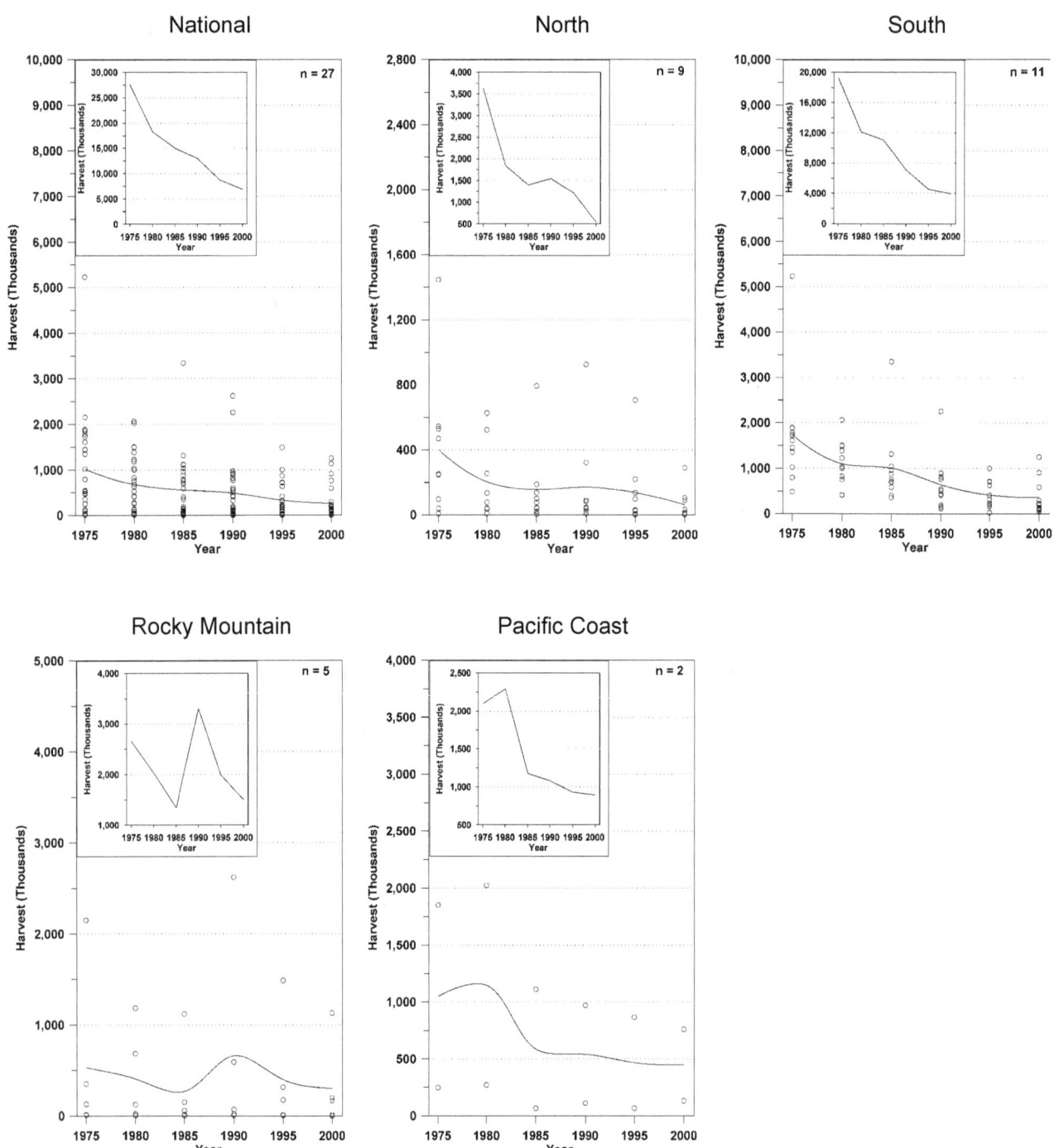

Figure 5. (Continued)

Prairie grouse

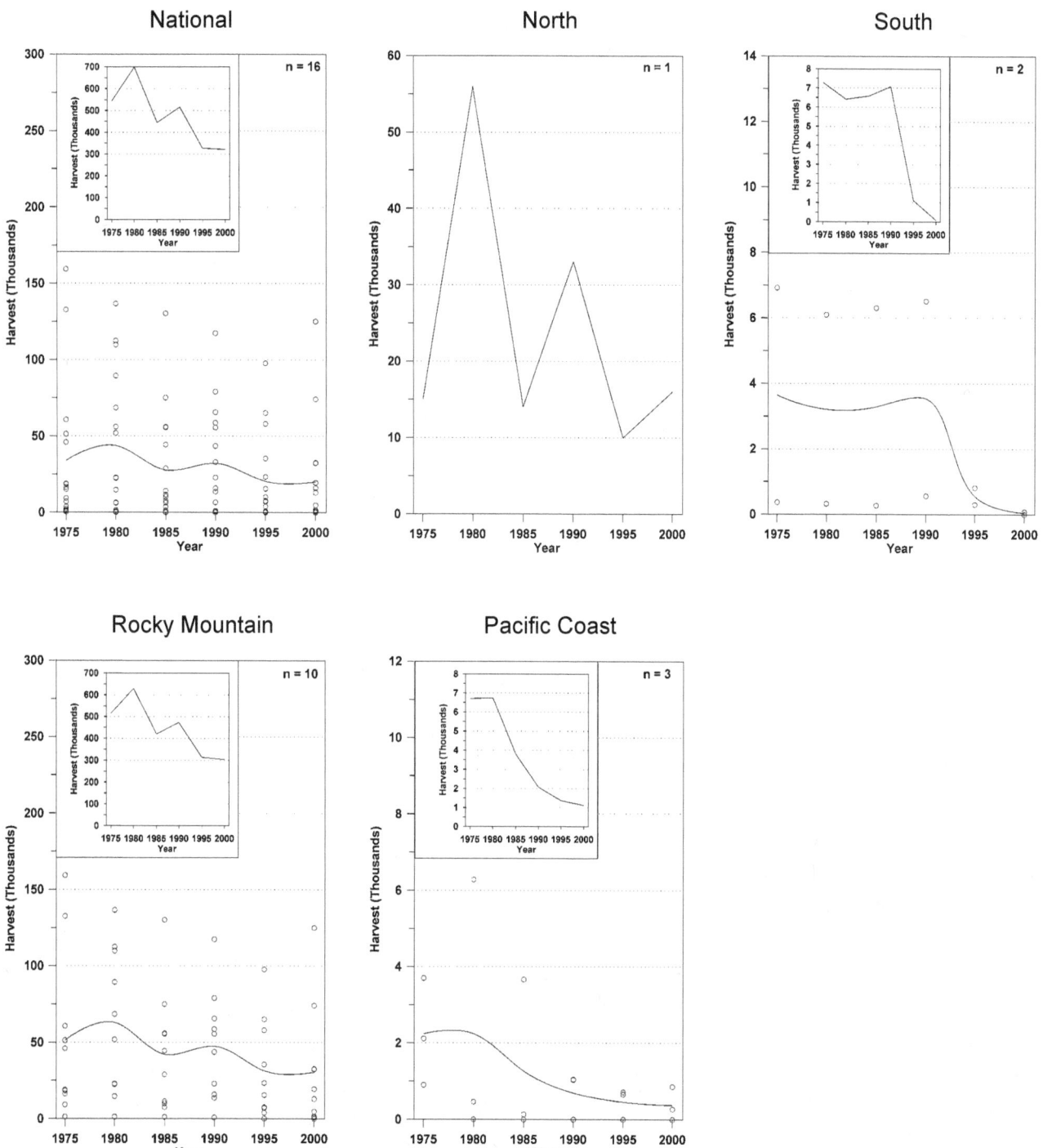

USDA Forest Service Gen. Tech. Rep. RMRS-GTR-219. 2009

25

Figure 5. (Continued)

Western quail

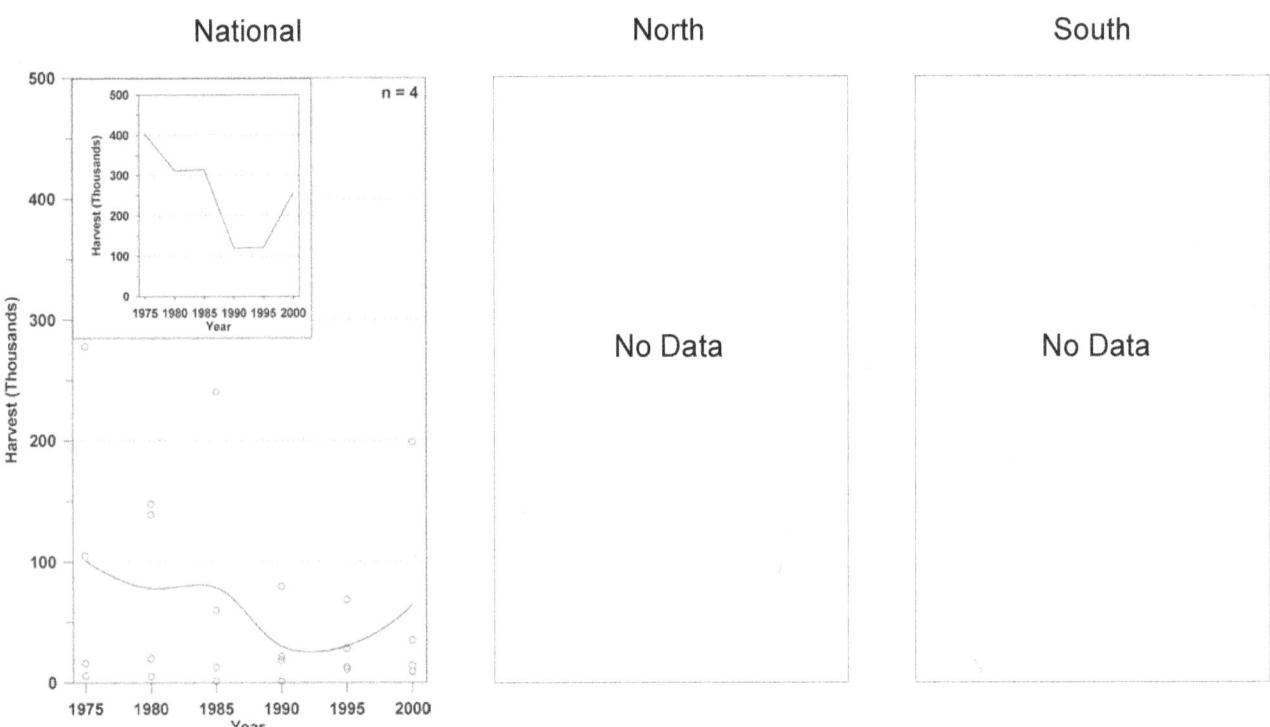

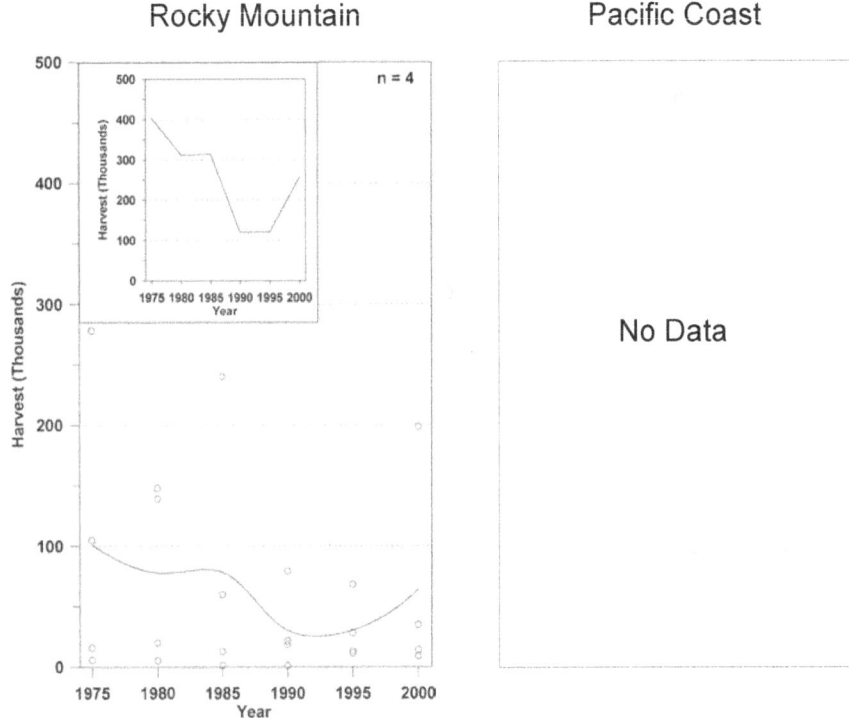

Big game population trends within RPA regions are, for the most part, qualitatively consistent with the patterns observed nationally (fig. 2). Exceptions to this observation include pronghorn in the South (which has shown steady declines since 1985 within two reporting states) and big game species in the Pacific Coast region generally (where populations have either remained relatively stable [elk, black bear] or have shown evidence of recent declines [deer, pronghorn]). The trends for deer in the Rocky Mountain region also deviate from the national pattern, with numbers remaining relatively stable near 1.25 million animals since 1985. In the case of deer, the noted deviation between regional and national trends in the case of the Rocky Mountain and Pacific Coast regions reflects the trend tied to mule deer and a much reduced contribution from white-tailed deer whose population and harvest estimates dominate the national statistics. It is also worth noting that regional trends deviating from the national pattern are often based on few reporting states indicating that the trends within that region may not reflect the trends across the entire species' geographic range.

The number of states contributing harvest data for big game species is more complete than population statistics. A total of 45 states contributed deer harvest data while 13 states contributed elk harvest numbers (fig. 3). National harvest trends over the 1975-2000 period have tended to mirror population trends. As with population statistics, wild turkey has undergone the greatest relative increase (+375 percent) among 40 states, while deer have undergone the greatest absolute increase (+4.9 million individuals) among 45 states. The only species where national harvest trends deviate from the national population trends is pronghorn. Pronghorn harvests have declined by 15 percent since 1975 and by 40 percent since peak harvests during the mid-1980s and early-1990s.

Regional harvest trends (fig. 3) also tend to mirror regional population trends. Wild turkey harvests have shown substantial increases in all four regions; deer and elk harvests have increased in all regions except the Pacific Coast; and black bear harvests have increased in all regions except the Rocky Mountains. Deviations in harvest trends relative to population trends were notable for pronghorn and black bear

in the Rocky Mountain region where harvests have declined (only slightly for black bear) for both species despite population increases.

Small Game Population and Harvest From State Agency Data

Many fewer states provided estimates of small game populations (fig. 4). A total of 5 states provided population estimates of northern bobwhite for the 1975-2000 period, while for hare, western quail, and prairie grouse, no state provided a sufficient set of population estimates to support an analysis of trends over the entire 25-year period. Consequently, the results for small game population trends have a high level of uncertainty associated with them.

Populations of northern bobwhite, the species with the greatest number of reporting states, have shown a monotonic decline in numbers since the mid-1970s (fig. 4). Populations within the 5 reporting states have declined by more than 85 percent. The only other species group with evidence of declines since 1975 is the forest grouse (–3 percent). Squirrels show essentially no change from 1975 to 2000. However, since the mid-1980s squirrel populations have declined by 1/3. Ring-necked pheasants, at least within two reporting states, have undergone substantial population increases since the mid-1970s (+190 percent). Cottontails show stability over the long term but there was recent evidence for declines following a population increase in 1990.

Small game harvest statistics are more completely reported with more than 15 states providing estimates for ring-necked pheasant, prairie and forest grouse, northern bobwhite, squirrel, and cottontail. Harvest trends (fig. 5) for small game diverge dramatically from the population trends reported earlier. All species and species groups show declining trends in small game harvests. The greatest declines occurred among hare (–86 percent), northern bobwhite (–75 percent), and cottontail (–69 percent). Regional trends in harvest are qualitatively consistent with the national trends with one exception — ring-necked pheasant harvests in the South have undergone monotonic increases since 1975 while all other regions show declines or stable harvests.

USDA Forest Service Gen. Tech. Rep. RMRS-GTR-219. 2009

27

Supplemental Population Trends From the North American Breeding Bird Survey

A total of 13 species defined as small upland game birds, and 1 big game bird species (wild turkey), are monitored by the BBS (table 2). Trends based on annual data from 1975 to 2000 appear to support the trends observed with the State Agency data. Wild turkey abundance has increase at an average annual rate of about 13.6 percent and is the only game bird within the suite of species we considered that shows evidence of statistically significant increase ($P < 0.001$) over this 25-year period. Other species with a positive trend include ruffed grouse, sharp-tailed grouse, and California quail; however, variation in their relative abundances is high enough such that these trends cannot be considered different from a population exhibiting stable abundances over this period. Species with at least marginally significantly ($P < 0.1$) declining trends include gray partridge, ring-necked pheasant, blue grouse, and northern bobwhite. As was observed in the State Agency data, the BBS confirms that the northern bobwhite has undergone substantial population declines with an average annual decline of 3.6 percent.

More recent trends (2000-2005) in upland game birds do deviate from the long-term trends in relative abundance. In particular, there is a tendency for the relative abundances to show a more prevalent pattern of qualitative increases as indicated by the sign on the trend coefficient (table 2). Eight species that showed negative trends in the long term were estimated to have positive trends since 2000; and six of those species (ring-necked pheasant, chukar, blue grouse, mountain quail, scaled quail, and Gambel's quail) had statistically significant ($P < 0.05$) positive trends. Only the wild turkey showed strong patterns of increase in both time periods with recent annual gains estimated at >9 percent per year. The greater prairie-chicken continued its long-term decline with an annual loss estimated at more than 9.5 percent since 2000.

Discussion

Population and harvest estimates from State Agencies are derived from a variety of approaches (Carpenter and others 2003, Mason and others 2006, Morellet and others 2007). The absence of any inventory design consistency among states makes regional inferences on population or harvest trends uncertain. Furthermore, for many of the species (particularly small game) states no longer provide population estimates. Because of these uncertainties we have tried to place emphasis on the qualitative trends rather than the actual magnitude of the estimates from each state. The variation in inventory methodologies among States notwithstanding, national

Table 2—Trends (percent/year) in breeding bird species from 1975-2000 from the North American Breeding Bird Survey (http://www.mbr-pwrc.usgs.gov/bbs/trend/tf03.html).

Species	Trend (1975-2000)			Trend (2000-2005)		
	N (routes)	Trend estimate (%/year)	P-value	N (routes)	Trend estimate (%/year)	P-value
Gray partridge (*Perdix perdix*)	156	−2.39	0.068	40	−1.65	0.861
Ring-necked pheasant (*Phasianus colchicus*)	1071	−0.82	0.015	697	2.86	0.002
Chukar (*Alectoris chukar*)	58	−6.13	0.367	44	10.72	0.004
Ruffed grouse (*Bonasa umbellus*)	274	1.17	0.318	82	−3.31	0.437
Sage grouse (*Centrocercus urophasianus*)	56	−2.59	0.317	28	22.93	0.224
Blue grouse (*Dendragapus obscurus*)	45	−3.63	0.047	31	24.41	0.001
Sharp-tailed grouse (*Tympanuchus phasianellus*)	76	1.24	0.649	43	6.61	0.209
Greater prairie-chicken (*Tympanuchus cupido*)	31	−5.75	0.111	21	−9.80	0.095
Mountain quail (*Oreortyx pictus*)	124	−0.28	0.701	95	8.22	0.032
Scaled quail (*Callipepla squamata*)	139	−0.23	0.914	89	12.19	0.004
California quail (*Callipepla californica*)	296	0.62	0.347	207	10.81	<0.001
Gambel's quail (*Callipepla gambelii*)	93	−1.14	0.221	64	10.49	<0.001
Northern bobwhite (*Colinus virginianus*)	1439	−3.58	<0.001	975	0.62	0.346
Wild turkey (*Meleagris gallopavo*)	705	13.65	<0.001	710	9.02	<0.001

population trend estimates from the BBS were consistent with State Agency derived trends over similar time periods. Although the BBS only permitted a comparison among avian species, it was reassuring that trends derived from a statistically rigorous survey procedure were consistent with trends compiled from State data.

Comparisons of the trends reported here with the literature among mammalian species also tended to offer a consistent assessment of recent trends. Peek (1995) concluded that elk now occupy more suitable habitat and are more numerous than at any time since the turn of the Twentieth Century. Similar conclusions have also been reached for white-tailed deer where empirical population estimates around 2000 suggest that deer numbers have grown to unprecedented levels (McCabe and McCabe 1997, Côté and others 2004). A comparison of our pronghorn population trends with those from Yoakum (2004) required a more detailed analysis. Yoakum (2004:86) reports a 20 percent decline in pronghorn numbers from 1989 to 1999. Over the 1990-2000 period, our data showed a 3.7 percent increase. Reconciling these discrepancies required consideration of the set of states contributing to Yoakum's analysis (17 states) and our analysis (11 states). Five out of the six states included in Yoakum (2004), but not included in our analysis, were states with small pronghorn populations that together contributed < 5 percent to the total count estimated for the United States. Pronghorn counts in those five states did little to explain the noted discrepancy. The sixth state (Montana) accounted for nearly 31 percent of the total pronghorn population estimate for 1989 reported in Yoakum (2004); and numbers in Montana plummeted more than 74 percent by 1999. If we ignore Montana's contribution to Yoakum's estimate, then the 1989 to 1999 trend indicated by his data was a 2.8 percent increase. This increase in pronghorn numbers is now in line with our reported population trend of +3.7 percent over a similar period of time. This reconciliation points to an important caveat when comparing across published accounts of big game population trends. Namely, that variation in the set of states contributing to the total population count can greatly affect the overall assessment of population trend due to regional variation in factors affecting reproduction and survivorship.

Consistency with the literature is not restricted to ungulates. Vaughn and Pelton (1995) found that 27 of 40 states reported increasing black bear populations around the mid-1990s. A more recent assessment of black bear population status conducted by Garshelis and Hristienko (2006) found that out of 51 U.S. state and Canadian provinces surveyed, no agency reported declining trends in black bear numbers and half reported at least slight increases from 1988-1999. Although the data used in several of these examples are derived from the same sources we used here, this consistency of pattern, at least qualitatively, suggests that the trends we report from State Agency data can't simply be dismissed because of the inherent idiosyncrasies embedded in a process that involves a compilation from 50 states.

The trends reported here do indicate that big game and small game populations and harvests differ in a very fundamental way. Big game populations and harvests reported here have, with a few exceptions, increased from 1975 to 2000. In several cases those increases have been substantial (e.g., population and harvests of wild turkey and deer). The trends for small game species diverge greatly from those reported for big game. The consistency of the divergence is not observable with the state-derived population data because so few states provided population estimates of small game species. The deviation is based on the consistent declines in small game harvests and the abundance trends among game birds derived from the BBS. A simple estimate of percentage change in harvests from 1975 to 2000 showed that on average (across the 9 species groups, unweighted for differences in harvest size) small game harvests declined by 49 percent. Whether these harvest trends reflect the population status of these species is debatable. Harvests can change for a number of reasons that are potentially independent of population levels including changes in the accessibility of land for hunting, changes in species preferences that hunters pursue, or changes in the number of days devoted to hunting. However, the trends derived from the BBS suggest that the cause of harvest declines among small game may have a component that is attributable to the populations of these species. Four of the five species with at least marginal evidence ($P \leq 0.1$) for a statistically significant trend during the 1975-2000

USDA Forest Service Gen. Tech. Rep. RMRS-GTR-219. 2009

29

period (table 2) were declining. The one species with significantly increasing populations — wild turkey — was classified as big game in this report.

Within species classified as small game, there also appears to be evidence that declines are prominent among those species associated with grassland, early successional, and farmland habitats. Three of the five species with the greatest percent decline in harvests (fig. 5) are clearly associated with grassland and agricultural habitats (northern bobwhite, cottontail, and prairie grouse). This pattern was substantiated by BBS-derived trends (table 2), with three out of the four small game species having evidence of at least marginally significant declines being associated with grassland/agricultural systems (gray partridge, ring-necked pheasant, and northern bobwhite).

Our purpose here was to review recent trends in big game and small game population and harvest trends. The motivation for this review stems ultimately from the mandates specified by the RPA. Moreover, because formal geographically extensive inventories for these species groups are lacking, it is important to update these trends periodically from state agency sources, even if they are derived from methodologies that vary widely, to indicate any important qualitative changes that have occurred so that natural resource managers and policymakers can consider this information during the decision-making process. The trends documented in this update show a continuation of trends that have been documented over the past two major wildlife assessments (Flather and Hoekstra 1989, Flather and others 1999). Big game population and harvest trends have to be considered, in general, a favorable resource situation. We don't mean to imply that population increases of game species are free of potentially negative consequences to ecosystems, local economies, and wildlife management. Habitats have limits on their capacity to sustainably support individuals and there is evidence that some species may be exceeding those limits (Levy 2006). Deer abundance has become problematic in many regions of the country and it remains an important management problem that still requires action (Warren 1997, Côté and others 2004). Because big game populations have generally shown long-term increases, the capacity for habitats and the public's desire to sustain those population levels represents an uncertain, if not an

emerging unfavorable, resource issue deserving of closer scientific and management scrutiny (Levy 2006). Small game species, particularly those associated with grassland and agricultural systems, show very little sign of long-term recovery from the declines noted in the 1990 Assessment (Flather and Hoekstra 1989). While there is local evidence that small game species can respond favorably to geographically extensive land use policies that provide suitable habitat (see Heard and others 2000), these local benefits have not, as yet, translated into observable sustained population and harvest benefits at regional and national scales. For this reason, the trends in small game population and harvest remain an important unresolved management issue of concern.

Monitoring that leads to unbiased and precise estimates of population size and harvest is fundamental to effective management of wildlife resources (Williams and others 2002). Estimating population and harvest of birds and mammals over large geographic areas is a conceptually simple idea; however, the inventories upon which those estimates are based are logistically difficult and expensive to implement (Morellet and others 2007). These difficulties notwithstanding, there is a need to improve monitoring protocols, data-sharing mechanisms, and species designations (that is, minimize lumping across species) such that our understanding of population fluctuations among harvested wildlife can inform management activities designed to affect harvest allocation or habitat restoration (Mason and others 2006). Failure to improve our capability to monitor populations and harvests can expose agencies to challenges from stakeholder groups that take time and money to resolve, and can erode trust among professional and citizen groups with an interest in the management and use of wildlife resources (see for example Freddy and others 2004). Furthermore, focused efforts on improving population monitoring should also consider comparability across state boundaries. Certainly, the authority to manage the species reviewed in this document rests largely with the states. However, ameliorating many of the pressures on these resources stemming from habitat loss and degradation, land use intensification, and climate change will require multi-jurisdictional (federal agencies, state agencies, and non-governmental organizations) and regional efforts that would benefit from monitoring data that can be aggregated easily across broad geographic areas. Realizing these monitoring improvements will come at a cost. There is a need to supplement monitoring budgets and to allocate the monitoring burden among those institutions that have a shared responsibility for wildlife resource stewardship to ensure that those who seek to hunt, observe, or photograph wildlife will continue to have the opportunity to enjoy these recreationally important species in the future.

References

Bystrak, D. 1981. The North American Breeding Bird Survey. Studies in Avian Biology 6: 34-41.

Carpenter, L. H.; Lutz, D.; Weybright, D. 2003. Mule deer data types, uses, analyses, and summaries. In: deVos, J. C., Jr.; Conover, M. R.; Headrick, N. E., eds. Mule deer conservation: issues and management strategies. Logan, UT: Berryman Institute Press, Utah State University: 163-175.

Cordell, H. K., principal author. 2004. Outdoor recreation for 21st century America: a report to the nation: the national survey on recreation and the environment. State College, PA: Venture Publishing. 293 p.

Côté, S. D.; Rooney, T. P.; Tremblay, J-P.; Dussault, C.; Waller, D. M. 2004. Ecological impacts of deer overabundance. Annual Review of Ecology, Evolution, and Systematics 35: 113-147.

Droege, S. 1990. The North American Breeding Bird Survey. In: Sauer, J. R.; Droege, S., eds. Survey design and statistical methods for estimation of avian population trends. Biol. Rep. 90(1). Washington, DC: USDI Fish and Wildlife Service: 1-4.

Erskine, A. J. 1978. The first ten years of the cooperative breeding bird survey in Canada. Canadian Wildlife Service Report Series. 42: 1-61.

Flather, C. H.; Brady, S. J.; Knowles, M. S. 1999. Wildlife resource trends in the United States: a technical document supporting the 2000 USDA Forest Service RPA Assessment. Gen. Tech. Rep. RMRS-GTR-33. Fort Collins, CO: U.S. Department of Agriculture, Forest Service, Rocky Mountain Research Station. 79 p.

Flather, C. H.; Hoekstra, T. W. 1989. An analysis of the wildlife and fish situation in the United States: 1989-2040. Gen. Tech. Rep. RM-178. Fort Collins, CO: U.S. Department of Agriculture, Rocky Mountain Forest and Range Experiment Station. 146 p.

Freddy, D. J.; White, G. C.; Kneeland, M. C.; Kahn, R. H.; Unsworth, J. W.; deVergie, W. J.; Graham, V. K.; Ellenberger, J. H.; Wagner, C. H. 2004. How many mule deer are there? Challenges of credibility in Colorado. Wildlife Society Bulletin 32: 916-927.

Garshelis, D. L.; Hristienko, H. 2006. State and provincial estimates of American black bear numbers versus assessments of population trend. Ursus 17: 1-7.

Geissler, P. H.; Noon, B. R. 1981. Estimates of avian population trends from the North American Breeding Bird Survey. Studies in Avian Biology 6: 42-51.

Geissler, P. H.; Sauer, J. R. 1990. Topics in route-regression analysis. In: Sauer, J. R.; Droege, S., eds. Survey design and statistical methods for estimation of avian population trends. Biol. Rep. 90(1). Washington, DC: USDI Fish and Wildlife Service: 54-57.

Golden Software, Inc. 2000. Grapher™ User's Guide. Graphing software for scientists and engineers. Golden, CO: Golden Software, Inc. 321 p.

Heard, L. P.; Allen, A. W.; Best, L. B.; Brady, S. J.; and others. 2000. A comprehensive review of farm bill contributions to wildlife conservation, 1985-2000. U.S. Department of Agriculture, Natural Resources Conservation Service, Wildlife Habitat Management Institute, Technical Report (USDA/NRCS/WHMI-2000). Washington, DC: U.S. Government Printing Office. 208 p.

Levy, S. 2006. A plague of deer. BioScience 56: 718-721.

Mason, R; Carpenter, L. H.; Cox, M.; deVos, J. C.; Fairchild, J.; Freddy, D. J.; Heffelfinger, J. R.; Kahn, R. H.; McCorquodale, S. M.; Pac, D. F.; Summers, D.; White, G. C.; Williams, B. K. 2006. A case for standardized ungulate surveys and data management in the western United States. Wildlife Society Bulletin 34: 1238-1242.

McCabe, T. R.; McCabe, R. E. 1997. Recounting whitetails past. In: McShea, W. J., Underwood, H. B.; Rappole, J. H., eds. The science of overabundance: deer ecology and population management. Washington, DC: Smithsonian Institute Press: 11-26.

Morellet, N.; Gaillard J-M.; Hewison, A. J. M.; Ballon, P.; Boscardin, Y.; Duncan, P.; Klein, F.; Maillard, D. 2007. Indicators of ecological change: new tools for managing populations of large herbivores. Journal of Applied Ecology 44: 634-643.

Peek, J. M. 1995. North American elk. In: LaRoe, E. T.; Farris, G. S.; Puckett, C. E.; Doran, P. D.; Mac, M. J., eds. Our living resources: a report to the nation on the distribution, abundance, and health of U.S. plants, animals, and ecosystems. Washington, DC: USDI, National Biological Service: 115-116.

Pollock, D. S. G. 1994. Smoothing with cubic splines. Paper No. 291. London: University of London, Queen Mary and Westfield College, Economics Department. 25 p.

Sauer, J. R.; Hines, J. E.; Fallon, J. 2007. The North American Breeding Bird Survey, results and analysis 1966-2006. Version 10.13.2007. USGS Patuxent Wildlife Research Center, Laurel, MD.

Sauer, J. R.; Peterjohn, B. G.; Link, W. A. 1994. Observer differences in the North American Breeding Bird Survey. Auk 111: 50-62.

Schoenberg, I. J. 1964. Spline functions and the problem of graduation. Proceedings of the National Academy of Sciences, USA 52:947-950.

USDI Fish and Wildlife Service; USDC Census Bureau. 2006. National survey of fishing, hunting, and wildlife-associated recreation. Washington, DC: U.S. Government Printing Office. 164 p.

USDA Forest Service Gen. Tech. Rep. RMRS-GTR-219. 2009

31

Vaughan, M. R.; Pelton, M. R. 1995. Black bears in North America. In: LaRoe, E. T.; Farris, G. S.; Puckett, C. E.; Doran, P. D.; Mac, M. J., eds. Our living resources: a report to the nation on the distribution, abundance, and health of U.S. plants, animals, and ecosystems. Washington, DC: USDI, National Biological Service: 100-103.

Warren, R. J., editor. 1997. The challenge of deer overabundance in the 21st century. Wildlife Society Bulletin 25: 213-214.

Williams, B. K.; Nichols, J. D.; Conroy, M. J. 2002. Analysis and management of animal populations. San Diego, CA: Academic Press. 817 p.

Yoakum, J. D. 2004. Distribution and abundance. In: O'Gara, B. W.; Yoakum, J. D., eds. Pronghorn: ecology and management. Boulder, CO: University Press of Colorado: 75-105.

Appendix: Data compilation instructions and an example data form sent to NRCS State Biologists for use in updating state-level big game and small game population and harvest statistics from State Wildlife Agencies.

```
                    HISTORICAL HARVEST AND POPULATION TRENDS

The purpose of this form is to update historical harvest and population data for commonly
harvested wildlife species in your state.  These data were acquired on previous requests to your
agency and we would like you to review the accuracy of those estimates, provide data where there
are historical information gaps, and provide more recent estimates of harvest and population
levels where applicable.  A description of the column headings on this form is displayed below.


COLUMN HEADING                       |  DESCRIPTION
-------------------------------------|---------------------------------------------------------
Common Name                          |  A description of the species name.  In some cases harvest
                                     |  and population information is presented for a group of
                                     |  species (e.g., deer, squirrels).  In this case harvest and
                                     |  population estimates should reflect all species composing
                                     |  the group.
                                     |
-------------------------------------|---------------------------------------------------------
                                     |
Species Code                         |  A 9- or 6-character code reflecting the first 3 letters of
                                     |  the genus, species, and subspecies (if applicable)
                                     |  name.  The code "SPP" appears if a species group
                                     |  name (e.g., deer, squirrels) is used.
                                     |
-------------------------------------|---------------------------------------------------------
                                     |
1975 Harvest/Population              |  Statewide harvest/population estimate representative of the
                                     |  year indicated.  These data were obtained from previous
1980 Harvest/Population              |  requests to your state agency.  Please review the accuracy of
                                     |  the estimates shown and provide estimates where there
1985 Harvest/Population              |  are historical gaps.  If data are not available for a
                                     |  particular year, then indicated by entering "ND".
1990 Harvest/Population              |
                                     |
-------------------------------------|---------------------------------------------------------
                                     |
1995 Harvest/Population              |  Provide statewide estimates of harvest and population for
                                     |  1995 and 2000.  If 2000 estimates are not available
1999/2000 Harvest/Population         |  then provide 1999.  Indicate the year of the data by
                                     |  underlining the appropriate year (use the underline option in
                                     |  your word processor).  If data are not available for a
                                     |  particular year, then indicate by entering "ND".
                                     |
-------------------------------------------------------------------------------------------------


The attached data file contains population and harvest data for your state.  Please review
and update those data and return to NRCS State Conservationist
```

USDA Forest Service Gen. Tech. Rep. RMRS-GTR-219. 2009

33

```
-------------------------------------- Data=Harvest --------------------------------------
```

Species	Species Code	1975 Totals	1980 Totals	1985 Totals	1990 Totals	1995 Totals	(UNDERLINE ONE) 2000/2001 Totals
Pronghorn	ANTAME	72	152	214	165	_____	_____
Bobwhite	COLVIR	2152250	1186000	1121000	2620000	_____	_____
Turkey, Wild	MELGAL	128	369	1998	5669	_____	_____
Deer, Mule	ODOHEM	1115	1869	2581	4000	_____	_____
Deer, White-tail	ODOVIR	4373	8434	23245	41000	_____	_____
Pheasant, Ring-necked	PHACOL	564000	972000	645000	742000	_____	_____
Squirrel	SCISPP	282000	273000	167000	141000	_____	_____
Cottontail	SYLSPP	371000	277000	317000	335000	_____	_____
Prairie-chicken, Greater	TYMCUP	16000	51000	54000	55000	_____	_____
Prairie-chicken, Lesser	TYMPAL	2300	900	1600	600	_____	_____

```
------------------------------------ Data=Population ------------------------------------
```

Species	Species Code	1975 Totals	1980 Totals	1985 Totals	1990 Totals	1995 Totals	(UNDERLINE ONE) 2000/2001 Totals
Pronghorn	ANTAME	926	1650	2000	1300	_____	_____
Turkey, Wild	MELGAL	2767	_____	70000	_____	_____	_____
Deer, Mule	ODOHEM	7640	50000	40000	_____	_____	_____
Deer, White-tail	ODOVIR	30560	10000	260000	_____	_____	_____
Pheasant, Ring-necked	PHACOL	1540000	_____	_____	_____	_____	_____
Prairie-chicken	TYMSPP	175754	_____	_____	_____	_____	_____